JUICE VITALITY

JUICING RECIPES FOR WELLNESS AND ENERGY

INDEX

DETOX DELIGHT

- 1 BEETROOT
- 2 CARROTS
- 1 SMALL CUCUMBER
- 1/2 LEMON, PEELED
- 1 INCH GINGER ROOT

1. WASH ALL INGREDIENTS THOROUGHLY.
2. PEEL THE BEETROOT AND GINGER ROOT.
3. CUT ALL INGREDIENTS INTO SIZES THAT FIT YOUR JUICER'S FEED.
4. JUICE ALL INGREDIENTS, STARTING WITH THE GINGER AND ENDING WITH THE CUCUMBER TO PUSH THROUGH ALL THE GINGER FLAVOR.
5. STIR AND ENJOY IMMEDIATELY.

ENERGY ELIXIR

- 2 LARGE APPLES
- 3 STALKS CELERY
- 1/2 CUP PINEAPPLE
- 1 HANDFUL SPINACH
- 1/2 LIME, PEELED

1. CLEAN AND PREPARE ALL INGREDIENTS.
2. CUT INTO SUITABLE SIZES.
3. START JUICING WITH SPINACH, FOLLOWED BY CELERY, APPLE, PINEAPPLE, AND FINALLY LIME.
4. ENJOY YOUR ENERGIZING DRINK!

IMMUNE BOOSTER

INGREDIENTS

- 3 ORANGES, PEELED
- 1/2 GRAPEFRUIT, PEELED
- 1/2 INCH TURMERIC ROOT
- 1/2 INCH GINGER ROOT
- A PINCH OF BLACK PEPPER

DIRECTIONS

1. PREPARE ALL INGREDIENTS, PEELING WHERE NECESSARY.
2. JUICE ALL INGREDIENTS TOGETHER, STARTING WITH TURMERIC AND GINGER.
3. ADD A PINCH OF BLACK PEPPER TO THE JUICE AND STIR WELL.
4. SERVE IMMEDIATELY FOR A VITAMIN C AND ANTI-INFLAMMATORY BOOST.

DIGESTIVE AID

- 1 APPLE
- 1/2 PAPAYA
- 1/2 INCH GINGER
- 1/2 LEMON, PEELED
- 1/4 TEASPOON CINNAMON

1. PREPARE INGREDIENTS, CLEANING AND CUTTING THEM AS NEEDED.
2. JUICE ALL THE INGREDIENTS TOGETHER.
3. STIR IN THE CINNAMON AFTER JUICING FOR ADDED DIGESTIVE BENEFITS.
4. DRINK TO AID DIGESTION.

ANTI-INFLAMMATORY POTION

INGREDIENTS

- 1 CUP PINEAPPLE
- 1/2 CUP BLUEBERRIES
- 1/2 INCH GINGER
- 1/2 INCH TURMERIC ROOT
- 1 TABLESPOON FLAXSEED OIL (ADD AFTER JUICING)

DIRECTIONS

1. PREP YOUR INGREDIENTS.
2. JUICE THE PINEAPPLE, BLUEBERRIES, GINGER, AND TURMERIC TOGETHER.
3. STIR IN THE FLAXSEED OIL INTO THE JUICE FOR OMEGA-3S AND ADDITIONAL ANTI-INFLAMMATORY BENEFITS.
4. SERVE THIS POWERFUL ANTI-INFLAMMATORY JUICE IMMEDIATELY.

SUNRISE SMOOTHIE

- 1 LARGE BANANA
- 1/2 CUP STRAWBERRIES
- 1/2 CUP ORANGE JUICE
- 1/2 CUP GREEK YOGURT
- 1 TEASPOON HONEY (OPTIONAL)

1. CLEAN AND PREPARE ALL INGREDIENTS.
2. CUT INTO SUITABLE SIZES FOR BLENDING.
3. START BLENDING WITH THE BANANA, FOLLOWED BY STRAWBERRIES, THEN ADD ORANGE JUICE AND GREEK YOGURT.
4. ADD HONEY FOR A TOUCH OF SWEETNESS IF DESIRED.
5. ENJOY YOUR REFRESHING DRINK!

GREEN CLEANSE COCKTAIL

INGREDIENTS

- 2 LARGE KALE LEAVES
- 1 CUP OF SPINACH
- 1 GREEN APPLE
- 2 STALKS OF CELERY
- 1/2 LEMON, PEELED
- 1 INCH OF GINGER ROOT

DIRECTIONS

1. CLEAN AND PREPARE ALL INGREDIENTS.
2. REMOVE TOUGH STEMS FROM KALE LEAVES IF NECESSARY. USE WHOLE SPINACH LEAVES.
3. QUARTER THE GREEN APPLE, REMOVING THE CORE. KEEP THE SKIN ON FOR EXTRA NUTRIENTS.
4. CHOP CELERY STALKS INTO PIECES SMALL ENOUGH TO FIT THROUGH YOUR JUICER.
5. PEEL THE LEMON TO AVOID BITTERNESS, LEAVING SOME WHITE PITH FOR NUTRIENTS.
6. PEEL THE GINGER ROOT; A SMALL PIECE ADDS FLAVOR AND HEALTH BENEFITS.
7. BEGIN JUICING BY ALTERNATING LEAFY GREENS WITH APPLE AND CELERY PIECES, FINISHING WITH LEMON AND GINGER.
8. STIR THE JUICE WELL AND SERVE IMMEDIATELY FOR MAXIMUM HEALTH BENEFITS.

LIVER LOVE POTION

- 1 BEETROOT
- 2 CARROTS
- 1 APPLE (PREFERABLY GREEN FOR LESS SWEETNESS)
- 1/2 LEMON, PEELED
- A SMALL HANDFUL OF DANDELION GREENS

1. CLEAN AND PREPARE ALL INGREDIENTS.
2. PEEL AND CHOP THE BEETROOT INTO CHUNKS.
3. WASH AND CHOP THE CARROTS; NO NEED TO PEEL IF ORGANIC.
4. CORE AND QUARTER THE APPLE, LEAVING THE SKIN ON.
5. PEEL THE LEMON TO REDUCE BITTERNESS.
6. WASH THE DANDELION GREENS THOROUGHLY.
7. BEGIN JUICING WITH THE DANDELION GREENS, THEN THE BEETROOT AND CARROTS, FOLLOWED BY THE APPLE, AND FINISH WITH THE LEMON FOR THE BEST FLAVOR BLEND.
8. STIR THE JUICE WELL AND ENJOY IMMEDIATELY FOR A DELICIOUS BOOST TO LIVER HEALTH.

REFRESHING CITRUS FLUSH

INGREDIENTS

- 1 GRAPEFRUIT
- 2 ORANGES
- 1/2 LEMON
- A FEW MINT LEAVES FOR AN EXTRA REFRESHING FLAVOR

DIRECTIONS

1. CLEAN AND PREPARE ALL INGREDIENTS.
2. PEEL THE GRAPEFRUIT, ORANGES, AND LEMON TO REMOVE THE BITTER OUTER LAYER. SEGMENT THEM TO FIT INTO YOUR JUICER.
3. WASH THE MINT LEAVES THOROUGHLY.
4. START JUICING WITH THE MINT LEAVES TO CAPTURE THEIR DELICATE FLAVORS, FOLLOWED BY THE CITRUS FRUITS.
5. GENTLY STIR THE JUICE TO EVENLY DISTRIBUTE THE MINTY ESSENCE.
6. ENJOY THIS VIBRANT, REFRESHING DRINK IMMEDIATELY FOR A DELIGHTFUL DETOX EXPERIENCE.

GINGER ZINGER

- 2 APPLES (GREEN FOR A LESS SWEET, MORE TART FLAVOR)
- 1 CARROT
- 1 INCH OF GINGER ROOT
- 1/4 TEASPOON OF TURMERIC POWDER (OR A 1/2 INCH TURMERIC ROOT IF AVAILABLE)

1. CLEAN AND PREPARE ALL INGREDIENTS.
2. CORE AND QUARTER THE APPLES; THERE'S NO NEED TO PEEL THEM.
3. WASH THE CARROT WELL; CHOP IT WITHOUT PEELING IF IT'S ORGANIC.
4. PEEL AND CHOP THE GINGER ROOT, ADJUSTING THE AMOUNT TO SUIT YOUR TASTE PREFERENCE.
5. IF USING FRESH TURMERIC, PEEL AND CHOP; IF USING POWDER, IT WILL BE ADDED AFTER JUICING.
6. BEGIN JUICING WITH THE GINGER AND CARROT TO CAPTURE THEIR BOLD FLAVORS, FOLLOWED BY THE APPLES, AND END WITH THE TURMERIC ROOT IF USING. STIR IN THE TURMERIC POWDER AFTER JUICING IF THAT'S WHAT YOU'RE USING.
7. STIR THE JUICE WELL TO ENSURE ALL ELEMENTS ARE FULLY INTEGRATED, ESPECIALLY IF TURMERIC POWDER IS USED.
8. ENJOY THIS VIBRANT, ZESTY JUICE RIGHT AWAY, TAKING ADVANTAGE OF ITS REFRESHING TASTE AND HEALTHFUL BENEFITS.

SWEET BEET DETOXIFIER

INGREDIENTS

- 1 MEDIUM BEETROOT
- 1/2 CUP PINEAPPLE, CHOPPED
- 1 SMALL CUCUMBER
- A FEW MINT LEAVES

DIRECTIONS

1. CLEAN AND PREPARE ALL INGREDIENTS.
2. PEEL AND CHOP THE BEETROOT INTO PIECES SUITABLE FOR JUICING.
3. PREPARE THE PINEAPPLE BY REMOVING THE SKIN AND CORE, THEN CHOPPING INTO PIECES THAT FIT YOUR JUICER.
4. CHOP THE CUCUMBER; PEEL IT FIRST IF IT'S NOT ORGANIC.
5. THE MINT LEAVES ARE READY AFTER A GOOD WASH; THERE'S NO NEED TO CHOP THEM.
6. BEGIN YOUR JUICING PROCESS WITH THE MINT LEAVES TO CAPTURE THEIR FLAVOR, THEN PROCEED WITH THE BEETROOT, PINEAPPLE, AND CUCUMBER. THE JUICY CUCUMBER AND PINEAPPLE WILL ENSURE ALL THE MINT FLAVOR IS EXTRACTED.
7. STIR THE JUICE WELL TO BLEND THE FLAVORS THOROUGHLY AND ENJOY IT IMMEDIATELY FOR A REFRESHING, DETOXIFYING EXPERIENCE.

TROPICAL CLEANSE

- 1 CUP PINEAPPLE, CHOPPED
- 1/2 CUP MANGO, CHOPPED
- JUICE OF 1 LIME
- 1 CUP COCONUT WATER

1. PREPARE ALL INGREDIENTS.
2. PEEL, CORE, AND CHOP THE PINEAPPLE INTO JUICER-FRIENDLY PIECES.
3. PEEL AND CHOP THE MANGO, REMOVING THE PIT.
4. JUICE THE LIME SEPARATELY AND SET ASIDE.
5. MEASURE OUT ONE CUP OF COCONUT WATER.
6. BEGIN BY JUICING THE PINEAPPLE AND MANGO TO EXTRACT AS MUCH JUICE AS POSSIBLE.
7. IN A LARGE PITCHER, COMBINE THE JUICES OF PINEAPPLE AND MANGO.
8. ADD THE LIME JUICE AND COCONUT WATER TO THE PITCHER, STIRRING WELL TO BLEND ALL THE INGREDIENTS.
9. SERVE YOUR TROPICAL CLEANISE IMMEDIATELY FOR A REFRESHING TASTE AND HYDRATION BOOST.

ANTIOXIDANT BLAST

- 1/2 CUP BLUEBERRIES
- 1/2 CUP BLACKBERRIES
- 1 CUP RED GRAPES
- 1/4 CUP ACAI BERRY JUICE

1. PREPARE ALL INGREDIENTS.
2. WASH THE BLUEBERRIES, BLACKBERRIES, AND RED GRAPES THOROUGHLY TO ENSURE THEY'RE CLEAN AND FREE FROM PESTICIDES. ORGANIC OPTIONS ARE BEST FOR HEALTH BENEFITS AND MINIMIZING TOXINS.
3. ENSURE RED GRAPES ARE STEMMED AND WASHED.
4. START THE JUICING PROCESS WITH THE GRAPES, AS THEIR HIGH WATER CONTENT HELPS EXTRACT MAXIMUM JUICE AND FLAVOR, FOLLOWED BY THE BLUEBERRIES AND BLACKBERRIES.
5. SINCE ACAI BERRY JUICE IS TYPICALLY PRE-MADE, ADD IT TO THE MIX AFTER THE OTHER FRUITS HAVE BEEN JUICED.
6. POUR THE FRESHLY JUICED FRUITS INTO A LARGE GLASS OR PITCHER, THEN ADD THE ACAI BERRY JUICE, STIRRING WELL TO COMBINE ALL THE INGREDIENTS INTO A POWERFUL, ANTIOXIDANT-RICH DRINK.
7. ENJOY YOUR ANTIOXIDANT BLAST RIGHT AWAY TO BENEFIT FROM ITS HEALTH-BOOSTING PROPERTIES, INCLUDING PROTECTION AGAINST OXIDATIVE STRESS AND INFLAMMATION.

HERBAL DETOX BLEND

- A SMALL HANDFUL OF PARSLEY
- A SMALL HANDFUL OF CILANTRO
- 1 LARGE CUCUMBER
- 2 STALKS OF CELERY
- 1 GREEN APPLE

1. PREPARE ALL INGREDIENTS.
2. THOROUGHLY WASH THE PARSLEY, CILANTRO, CUCUMBER, CELERY, AND GREEN APPLE. IT'S IMPORTANT TO CLEAN THE HERBS AND LEAFY GREENS CAREFULLY TO REMOVE ANY DIRT.
3. FOR THE PARSLEY AND CILANTRO, ENSURE THEY'RE CLEAN BUT NO NEED TO CHOP AS THEY CAN BE JUICED WHOLE.
4. CUT THE CUCUMBER INTO LENGTHS THAT FIT YOUR JUICER; PEEL IT FIRST IF IT'S NOT ORGANIC.
5. WASH AND CHOP THE CELERY INTO SHORTER LENGTHS SUITABLE FOR JUICING.
6. CORE AND QUARTER THE GREEN APPLE, LEAVING THE SKIN ON FOR EXTRA NUTRIENTS.
7. START THE JUICING PROCESS WITH THE PARSLEY AND CILANTRO TO CAPTURE THEIR VIBRANT FLAVORS AND HEALTH BENEFITS, FOLLOWED BY THE CUCUMBER AND CELERY FOR A HYDRATING EFFECT, AND FINISH WITH THE GREEN APPLE FOR A NATURAL SWEETNESS AND TO ENSURE ALL THE HERB FLAVORS ARE FULLY EXTRACTED.
8. STIR THE JUICE WELL TO COMBINE ALL THE FLAVORS EVENLY.
9. ENJOY YOUR HERBAL DETOX BLEND IMMEDIATELY TO TAKE FULL ADVANTAGE OF ITS CLEANSING AND REFRESHING BENEFITS. THIS DRINK IS NOT JUST A POTENT DETOXIFIER BUT ALSO A DELIGHTFUL REFRESHMENT FOR ANY TIME OF THE DAY.

SPICY LEMONADE CLEANSE

- JUICE OF 2 LEMONS
- 2 TABLESPOONS MAPLE SYRUP
- 1/10 TEASPOON CAYENNE PEPPER (ADJUST TO TASTE)
- 2 CUPS OF WATER (STILL OR SPARKLING)

1. PREPARE THE LEMONS BY CUTTING THEM IN HALF AND SQUEEZING THEIR JUICE INTO A PITCHER OR LARGE GLASS, MAKING SURE TO REMOVE ANY SEEDS.
2. ADD THE MAPLE SYRUP TO THE LEMON JUICE FOR SWEETNESS. INCORPORATE THE CAYENNE PEPPER NEXT, STARTING WITH A SMALLER AMOUNT IF YOU PREFER LESS SPICE, AND ADJUST ACCORDING TO YOUR TASTE.
3. POUR THE WATER INTO THE PITCHER, CHOOSING STILL OR SPARKLING WATER BASED ON YOUR PREFERENCE, AND STIR WELL TO MIX ALL THE INGREDIENTS THOROUGHLY.
4. YOU CAN ENJOY THE SPICY LEMONADE CLEANSE IMMEDIATELY OR CHILL IT IN THE REFRIGERATOR FOR A REFRESHING COLD DRINK. MAKE SURE TO STIR WELL BEFORE SERVING, ESPECIALLY IF THE DRINK HAS BEEN SITTING AND THE INGREDIENTS HAVE SETTLED.
5. SAVOR THIS SPICY LEMONADE CLEANSE EITHER THROUGHOUT THE DAY OR AS A MORNING RITUAL TO ACTIVATE YOUR METABOLISM AND SUPPORT YOUR BODY'S DETOXIFICATION PROCESS. THIS CONCOCTION IS NOT JUST A PALATE-PLEASING REFRESHMENT BUT ALSO AIDS IN YOUR OVERALL WELLNESS BY BOLSTERING THE BODY'S NATURAL CLEANSING SYSTEMS.

ALKALIZING GREEN JUICE

- 1 LARGE CUCUMBER
- 2 STALKS OF CELERY
- JUICE OF 1 LIME
- 1 CUP OF SPINACH LEAVES
- 1/2 AVOCADO

1. PREPARE ALL THE INGREDIENTS BY WASHING THEM THOROUGHLY. USE ORGANIC PRODUCE WHEN POSSIBLE TO REDUCE PESTICIDE EXPOSURE.
2. CHOP THE CUCUMBER TO FIT YOUR JUICER. PEEL IT FIRST IF IT'S NOT ORGANIC.
3. WASH AND CHOP THE CELERY INTO SHORTER LENGTHS THAT WILL EASILY GO THROUGH YOUR JUICER.
4. ENSURE THE SPINACH IS CLEAN AND READY TO USE.
5. JUICE THE LIME SEPARATELY AND SET ASIDE.
6. HALVE THE AVOCADO, REMOVE THE PIT, AND SCOOP OUT THE FLESH.
7. START YOUR JUICING PROCESS WITH THE CUCUMBER AND CELERY TO CREATE A HYDRATING BASE. FOLLOW WITH THE SPINACH, PLACING IT BETWEEN THE MORE WATERY CUCUMBER AND CELERY TO ENHANCE JUICE EXTRACTION.
8. TRANSFER THE JUICE TO A BLENDER, ADD THE AVOCADO AND LIME JUICE, AND BLEND UNTIL SMOOTH. THE AVOCADO ENRICHES THE JUICE WITH CREAMINESS AND HEALTHY FATS, AIDING IN THE ABSORPTION OF THE VITAMINS.
9. POUR THE ALKALIZING GREEN JUICE INTO A GLASS AND ENJOY IT RIGHT AWAY. THIS JUICE IS AN IDEAL CHOICE FOR A HEALTHY START TO YOUR DAY OR A REVITALIZING MID-DAY DRINK, PROMOTING YOUR BODY'S BALANCE AND HYDRATION.

MORNING SUNSHINE SMOOTHIE

INGREDIENTS

- 1/2 CUP ORANGE JUICE (PREFERABLY FRESH SQUEEZED FOR A VIBRANT START)
- 1/2 BANANA (FOR A SMOOTH, CREAMY TEXTURE)
- 1/2 CUP FROZEN MANGO CHUNKS (FOR TROPICAL SWEETNESS)
- 1/4 CUP CARROT JUICE (FOR A BOOST OF VITAMIN A AND A SUBTLE EARTHINESS)
- 1/2 TEASPOON FRESH GINGER (FOR A ZESTY KICK)
- A PINCH OF TURMERIC POWDER (FOR COLOR AND ANTI-INFLAMMATORY BENEFITS)
- A SMALL HANDFUL OF ICE CUBES (FOR A REFRESHING CHILL)

DIRECTIONS

1. PREPARE ALL INGREDIENTS: ENSURE THE BANANA IS PEELED AND GINGER IS FINELY GRATED. IF YOU'RE JUICING THE CARROT YOURSELF, DO SO AHEAD OF TIME.
2. BEGIN BY PLACING THE ORANGE JUICE, BANANA, FROZEN MANGO, CARROT JUICE, FRESH GINGER, AND TURMERIC IN A BLENDER.
3. ADD A SMALL HANDFUL OF ICE CUBES TO THE MIX.
4. BLEND UNTIL SMOOTH AND CREAMY, ENSURING THE GINGER AND TURMERIC ARE FULLY INTEGRATED.
5. TASTE AND ADJUST THE SWEETNESS OR GINGER ACCORDING TO YOUR PREFERENCE. IF YOU LIKE IT SWEETER, YOU CAN ADD A LITTLE HONEY OR MAPLE SYRUP.
6. SERVE THE MORNING SUNSHINE SMOOTHIE IMMEDIATELY IN A TALL GLASS. GARNISH WITH A SLICE OF ORANGE OR A SPRIG OF MINT FOR AN EXTRA TOUCH OF MORNING FRESHNESS.

GREEN POWER PUNCH

INGREDIENTS

- 2 LARGE KALE LEAVES
- 1 LARGE GREEN APPLE
- 1 LARGE CUCUMBER
- JUICE OF 1 LIME

DIRECTIONS

1. BEGIN BY WASHING ALL THE INGREDIENTS WELL. USING ORGANIC PRODUCE IS RECOMMENDED TO MINIMIZE THE INTAKE OF PESTICIDES AND CHEMICALS.
2. PREPARE THE KALE BY REMOVING THE STEMS IF THEY'RE TOO TOUGH. ROUGHLY CHOP THE LEAVES TO MAKE THEM EASIER TO JUICE.
3. CORE AND QUARTER THE GREEN APPLE. THERE'S NO NEED TO PEEL IT SINCE THE SKIN IS PACKED WITH NUTRIENTS.
4. CHOP THE CUCUMBER INTO PIECES THAT WILL FIT YOUR JUICER COMFORTABLY. IF IT'S ORGANIC, YOU CAN KEEP THE PEEL ON TO RETAIN ITS NUTRITIONAL BENEFITS.
5. JUICE THE LIME SEPARATELY TO ENSURE YOU CAN CONTROL THE AMOUNT OF ZEST ADDED TO THE PUNCH.
6. START JUICING WITH THE KALE LEAVES, AS THEY MIGHT NEED A BIT MORE EFFORT TO PROCESS. THEN, CONTINUE WITH THE GREEN APPLE AND CUCUMBER. THESE INGREDIENTS NOT ONLY COMPLEMENT THE KALE'S FLAVOR BUT ALSO ENSURE EFFICIENT JUICING, LEAVING NO WASTE BEHIND.
7. AFTER JUICING, MIX IN THE FRESHLY SQUEEZED LIME JUICE TO ADD A ZESTY TWIST TO YOUR GREEN POWER PUNCH.
8. SERVE THE JUICE IN A GLASS IMMEDIATELY TO ENJOY ITS FULL SPECTRUM OF FLAVORS AND HEALTH BENEFITS. THIS POWERHOUSE DRINK IS PERFECT FOR KICKSTARTING YOUR DAY OR AS A REVITALIZING PICK-ME-UP, OFFERING A BURST OF ENERGY AND ESSENTIAL NUTRIENTS.

BEETROOT BLAST

INGREDIENTS

- 1 MEDIUM BEETROOT
- 2 LARGE APPLES
- 2 LARGE CARROTS

DIRECTIONS

1. WASH ALL INGREDIENTS. IF ORGANIC, NO NEED TO PEEL; JUST CHOP TO FIT YOUR JUICER.
2. JUICE THE BEETROOT FIRST FOR ITS COLOR AND NUTRIENTS.
3. FOLLOW WITH CARROTS, THEN APPLES, TO ENSURE SMOOTH JUICING.
4. STIR WELL AND SERVE IMMEDIATELY FOR AN ENERGIZING DRINK.

TROPICAL ENERGY SURGE

- 1 CUP PINEAPPLE, CHOPPED
- 1 CUP MANGO, CHOPPED
- 1 CUP COCONUT WATER
- JUICE OF 1 LIME

1. PREPARE FRUITS: PEEL AND CHOP PINEAPPLE AND MANGO.
2. MEASURE 1 CUP OF COCONUT WATER.
3. JUICE THE LIME.
4. FOR JUICING: JUICE PINEAPPLE AND MANGO, THEN STIR IN COCONUT WATER AND LIME JUICE.
5. FOR BLENDING: BLEND PINEAPPLE, MANGO, AND COCONUT WATER UNTIL SMOOTH, THEN ADD LIME JUICE.
6. SERVE IMMEDIATELY IN A LARGE GLASS FOR A REFRESHING ENERGY BOOST.

BERRY BOOST SMOOTHIE

INGREDIENTS

- 1 CUP MIXED BERRIES (FRESH OR FROZEN)
- 1 RIPE BANANA
- 1 CUP ALMOND MILK
- OPTIONAL: 1 TABLESPOON HONEY OR MAPLE SYRUP FOR SWEETNESS

DIRECTIONS

1. IF USING FRESH BERRIES, WASH THEM. NO NEED FOR ICE IF USING FROZEN BERRIES.
2. PEEL THE BANANA AND BREAK IT INTO CHUNKS.
3. COMBINE BERRIES, BANANA CHUNKS, AND ALMOND MILK IN A BLENDER. ADD HONEY OR MAPLE SYRUP FOR EXTRA SWEETNESS, IF DESIRED.
4. BLEND UNTIL SMOOTH. ADJUST THICKNESS WITH MORE ALMOND MILK IF NEEDED.
5. SERVE IMMEDIATELY IN YOUR FAVORITE GLASS.

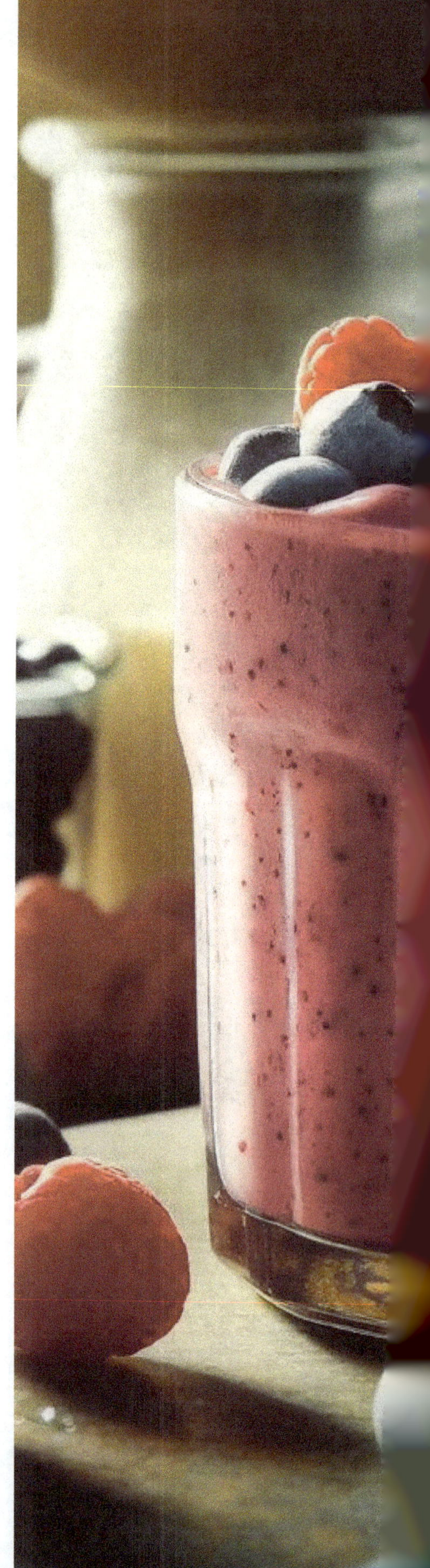

CITRUS ZING

INGREDIENTS

- 1 LARGE GRAPEFRUIT
- 2 LARGE ORANGES
- A SMALL HANDFUL OF FRESH MINT LEAVES

DIRECTIONS

1. PEEL GRAPEFRUIT AND ORANGES, REMOVING SEEDS. RETAIN THE WHITE PITH FOR NUTRIENTS IF JUICING, BUT REMOVE IF SENSITIVE TO BITTERNESS.
2. WASH MINT LEAVES THOROUGHLY.
3. FOR JUICING: JUICE MINT LEAVES FIRST, THEN GRAPEFRUIT AND ORANGES TO CAPTURE ALL FLAVORS.
4. FOR BLENDING: BLEND CITRUS FRUITS, STRAIN TO REMOVE PULP, AND MUDDLE MINT IN THE JUICE OR BLEND A FEW LEAVES WITH THE FRUITS.
5. STIR WELL AND SERVE CHILLED FOR A REFRESHING, MINT-INFUSED CITRUS DRINK.

POMEGRANATE POWER

- SEEDS FROM 1 LARGE POMEGRANATE
- 2 LARGE RED APPLES
- JUICE OF 1/2 LEMON

1. REMOVE POMEGRANATE SEEDS, PREFERABLY IN WATER TO AVOID SPLATTER.
2. CORE AND CHOP APPLES INTO CHUNKS, KEEPING THE SKIN ON.
3. JUICE THE LEMON HALF, DISCARDING ANY SEEDS.
4. JUICE POMEGRANATE SEEDS FIRST, THEN APPLE CHUNKS. IF NEEDED, BLEND AND STRAIN POMEGRANATE SEEDS FOR JUICE.
5. STIR IN LEMON JUICE FOR A ZESTY TOUCH.
6. MIX WELL AND SERVE IMMEDIATELY FOR A BURST OF NATURAL ENERGY AND ANTIOXIDANTS.

WATERMELON WAKE-UP

- 2 CUPS WATERMELON, CUBED AND SEEDS REMOVED
- 1 CUP STRAWBERRIES, HULLED
- 1 MEDIUM CUCUMBER, PEELED IF NOT ORGANIC

1. WASH STRAWBERRIES THOROUGHLY AND HULL THEM.
2. CHOP THE CUCUMBER INTO SMALLER PIECES. PEEL IF NOT ORGANIC.
3. FOR JUICING: BEGIN WITH CUCUMBER, FOLLOWED BY STRAWBERRIES, AND END WITH WATERMELON TO ENSURE ALL FLAVORS BLEND WELL.
4. FOR BLENDING: COMBINE ALL INGREDIENTS IN A BLENDER UNTIL SMOOTH. OPTIONALLY, STRAIN TO REMOVE PULP FOR A SMOOTHER DRINK, BUT RETAINING IT ADDS FIBER.
5. SERVE CHILLED OR IMMEDIATELY OVER ICE FOR A REFRESHING AND HYDRATING BOOST.

MINTY MELON ENERGIZER

INGREDIENTS

- 2 CUPS HONEYDEW MELON, CUBED
- 1 LARGE CUCUMBER
- A HANDFUL OF FRESH MINT LEAVES

DIRECTIONS

1. PREPARE THE HONEYDEW MELON BY REMOVING SEEDS AND RIND, THEN CUBE THE FLESH. USE A RIPE MELON FOR SWEETNESS.
2. IF ORGANIC, LEAVE THE CUCUMBER SKIN ON; OTHERWISE, PEEL AND CHOP IT.
3. WASH MINT LEAVES THOROUGHLY.
4. FOR JUICING: BEGIN WITH MINT LEAVES, THEN CUCUMBER, AND FINISH WITH HONEYDEW MELON TO BLEND ALL FLAVORS.
5. FOR BLENDING: COMBINE ALL INGREDIENTS IN A BLENDER, ADD WATER OR ICE IF NEEDED FOR DESIRED CONSISTENCY.
6. SERVE IMMEDIATELY IN GLASSES FOR A HYDRATING AND REFRESHING BOOST.

AVOCADO GREEN TEA SMOOTHIE

INGREDIENTS

- 1 RIPE AVOCADO
- 1 CUP FRESH SPINACH LEAVES
- 1 TEASPOON MATCHA GREEN TEA POWDER
- 1-2 TEASPOONS HONEY (TO TASTE)
- 1 CUP ALMOND MILK (OR PREFERRED MILK)

DIRECTIONS

1. HALVE THE AVOCADO, REMOVE THE PIT, AND SCOOP OUT THE FLESH.
2. WASH SPINACH LEAVES THOROUGHLY.
3. MEASURE MATCHA POWDER, ENSURING IT'S HIGH QUALITY FOR FLAVOR AND BENEFITS.
4. ADJUST HONEY TO YOUR SWEETNESS PREFERENCE.
5. MEASURE OUT ALMOND MILK, OR SUBSTITUTE WITH YOUR CHOICE OF MILK.
6. COMBINE ALL INGREDIENTS IN A BLENDER.
7. BLEND UNTIL SMOOTH AND CREAMY, ADDING MORE ALMOND MILK OR WATER IF NEEDED FOR CONSISTENCY.
8. SERVE IMMEDIATELY IN A GLASS FOR A NUTRIENT-RICH ENERGY BOOST.

BERRY ANTIOXIDANT SUPREME SMOOTHIE

- 1/2 CUP BLUEBERRIES (FRESH OR FROZEN)
- 1/2 CUP STRAWBERRIES, HULLED (FRESH OR FROZEN)
- 1/2 CUP RASPBERRIES (FRESH OR FROZEN)
- 1 RIPE BANANA, PEELED AND SLICED
- 1 CUP SPINACH LEAVES, WASHED
- 1 TABLESPOON CHIA SEEDS (FOR A BOOST OF FIBER AND OMEGA-3 FATTY ACIDS)
- 1 CUP ALMOND MILK (UNSWEETENED) OR ANY MILK OF YOUR CHOICE
- OPTIONAL: A TEASPOON OF HONEY OR MAPLE SYRUP FOR ADDED SWEETNESS

1. IF USING FROZEN BERRIES, THERE'S NO NEED TO ADD ICE, WHICH MAKES THIS SMOOTHIE PERFECT FOR A COLD, REFRESHING TREAT.
2. PLACE THE BLUEBERRIES, STRAWBERRIES, RASPBERRIES, AND BANANA IN THE BLENDER.
3. ADD THE SPINACH LEAVES ON TOP OF THE FRUIT. THIS LAYERING HELPS BLEND THE INGREDIENTS SMOOTHLY.
4. SPRINKLE THE CHIA SEEDS INTO THE BLENDER.
5. POUR IN THE ALMOND MILK. IF YOU PREFER A THINNER SMOOTHIE, YOU CAN ADD MORE MILK OR A LITTLE WATER.
6. BLEND ON HIGH UNTIL ALL THE INGREDIENTS ARE THOROUGHLY COMBINED AND THE SMOOTHIE HAS A SMOOTH, CREAMY TEXTURE.
7. TASTE THE SMOOTHIE. IF YOU PREFER IT A BIT SWEETER, ADD HONEY OR MAPLE SYRUP TO TASTE, THEN BLEND AGAIN BRIEFLY.
8. SERVE THE BERRY ANTIOXIDANT SUPREME SMOOTHIE IMMEDIATELY, GARNISHED WITH A FEW WHOLE BERRIES ON TOP FOR A BEAUTIFUL PRESENTATION.

GREEN DEFENSE

- 1 CUP SPINACH LEAVES
- 1 CUP KALE LEAVES, STEMS REMOVED
- 1 GREEN APPLE, CORED AND SLICED
- JUICE OF 1 LEMON
- A PINCH OF ECHINACEA POWDER

1. WASH SPINACH AND KALE LEAVES THOROUGHLY.
2. CORE AND SLICE THE GREEN APPLE, LEAVING THE SKIN ON FOR EXTRA NUTRIENTS.
3. JUICE THE LEMON SEPARATELY, ENSURING NO SEEDS GET INTO THE JUICE.
4. BEGIN JUICING WITH KALE AND SPINACH FOR THEIR RICH VITAMIN AND MINERAL CONTENT.
5. ADD GREEN APPLE SLICES NEXT FOR SWEETNESS AND TO AID IN JUICING THE GREENS.
6. STIR LEMON JUICE INTO THE MIXTURE FOR A VITAMIN C BOOST.
7. MIX IN A PINCH OF ECHINACEA POWDER FOR ITS IMMUNE-SUPPORTING BENEFITS.
8. SERVE THE GREEN DEFENSE IMMEDIATELY FOR MAXIMUM FRESHNESS AND HEALTH BENEFITS, PERFECT FOR A MORNING BOOST OR AN AFTERNOON PICK-ME-UP.

ANTIOXIDANT ADVENTURE

INGREDIENTS

- 1 CUP BLUEBERRIES
- 1 CUP BLACKBERRIES
- 1 CUP POMEGRANATE SEEDS (FROM ABOUT 1 MEDIUM POMEGRANATE)

DIRECTIONS

1. WASH BLUEBERRIES AND BLACKBERRIES THOROUGHLY. USE FRESH BERRIES FOR PEAK NUTRITION, BUT FROZEN ARE FINE IF THAT'S WHAT'S AVAILABLE.
2. HALVE THE POMEGRANATE AND REMOVE THE SEEDS IN A BOWL OF WATER TO AVOID SPLATTERS AND EASE SEPARATION.
3. FOR JUICING: JUICE BLUEBERRIES, BLACKBERRIES, AND THEN POMEGRANATE SEEDS IN THAT ORDER FOR A BLEND RICH IN ANTIOXIDANTS.
4. WITHOUT A JUICER: BLEND ALL FRUITS WITH A BIT OF WATER, THEN STRAIN TO EXTRACT THE JUICE.
5. STIR JUICES TOGETHER WELL AND SERVE IMMEDIATELY TO ENJOY THE FULL SPECTRUM OF HEALTH BENEFITS.

GINGER TURMERIC TONIC

- 2 INCHES OF GINGER ROOT, PEELED
- 1 INCH OF TURMERIC ROOT, PEELED (OR 1/2 TEASPOON TURMERIC POWDER)
- 4 LARGE CARROTS, WASHED
- 2 APPLES, CORED AND SLICED
- 1 TABLESPOON AGAVE NECTAR (ADJUST TO TASTE)

1. PREPARE THE INGREDIENTS:
   - GINGER AND TURMERIC ROOT: PEEL AND CHOP INTO SMALLER PIECES. FRESH ROOTS ARE PREFERRED FOR THEIR POTENCY AND FLAVOR, BUT TURMERIC POWDER CAN BE USED AS A SUBSTITUTE IF FRESH TURMERIC ISN'T AVAILABLE.
   - CARROTS: NO NEED TO PEEL IF THEY'RE ORGANIC, JUST WASH THEM THOROUGHLY. CHOP INTO JUICER-FRIENDLY SIZES.
   - APPLES: CORE AND SLICE. KEEPING THE SKIN ON WILL ADD ADDITIONAL NUTRIENTS.
2. START WITH THE GINGER AND TURMERIC TO ENSURE THEIR FLAVORS INFUSE INTO THE JUICE. FOLLOW WITH THE CARROTS AND APPLES, WHICH WILL ADD SWEETNESS AND HELP PUSH THROUGH ALL THE SPICY FLAVORS FROM THE GINGER AND TURMERIC.
3. STIR IN THE AGAVE NECTAR INTO THE JUICE MIXTURE AFTER JUICING. ADJUST THE SWEETNESS ACCORDING TO YOUR PREFERENCE, KEEPING IN MIND THAT THE AGAVE'S MILD FLAVOR COMPLEMENTS THE SPICY NOTES OF THE TONIC BEAUTIFULLY.
4. SERVE: ENJOY THE GINGER TURMERIC TONIC IMMEDIATELY, SERVING IT AT ROOM TEMPERATURE OR SLIGHTLY CHILLED, DEPENDING ON YOUR PREFERENCE. THIS TONIC IS NOT JUST A TREAT FOR THE TASTE BUDS BUT ALSO A HEALTHFUL ELIXIR THAT SUPPORTS IMMUNE FUNCTION, DIGESTION, AND OVERALL WELL-BEING.

CARROT COMFORT

INGREDIENTS

- 4 LARGE CARROTS, WASHED AND CHOPPED
- 1 INCH OF GINGER ROOT, PEELED
- 2 LARGE APPLES, CORED AND SLICED
- 1/2 TEASPOON TURMERIC POWDER (OR 1 INCH OF FRESH TURMERIC ROOT, PEELED)

DIRECTIONS

1. PREPARE CARROTS BY WASHING AND CHOPPING INTO PIECES THAT EASILY FIT YOUR JUICER.
2. PEEL GINGER AND TURMERIC ROOT (IF USING FRESH). THESE SPICES OFFER ANTI-INFLAMMATORY BENEFITS AND AID DIGESTION.
3. CORE AND SLICE APPLES. THEIR NATURAL SWEETNESS AND FIBER ENHANCE THE JUICE'S FLAVOR AND HEALTHINESS.
4. JUICE GINGER AND TURMERIC FIRST FOR THEIR FLAVORS AND BENEFITS, THEN ADD CARROTS, AND FINISH WITH APPLES TO ENSURE A THOROUGH BLEND.
5. STIR THE JUICE WELL TO COMBINE ALL FLAVORS. SERVE IMMEDIATELY TO ENJOY THE OPTIMAL TASTE AND NUTRITIONAL BENEFITS.

TROPICAL BLISS SMOOTHIE

INGREDIENTS

- 1 CUP PINEAPPLE, CHOPPED
- 1 CUP MANGO, CHOPPED
- 1 BANANA, SLICED
- 1/2 CUP COCONUT MILK (FOR THAT CREAMY TEXTURE AND TROPICAL FLAVOR)
- JUICE OF 1 LIME (FOR A ZESTY KICK)
- OPTIONAL: A TABLESPOON OF COCONUT FLAKES OR SHREDDED COCONUT FOR GARNISH
- OPTIONAL: A FEW ICE CUBES FOR AN EXTRA-CHILLED SMOOTHIE

DIRECTIONS

1. PREPARE THE FRUITS BY CHOPPING THE PINEAPPLE AND MANGO, AND SLICING THE BANANA.
2. ADD THE CHOPPED FRUITS TO A BLENDER ALONG WITH THE BANANA SLICES.
3. POUR IN THE COCONUT MILK FOR A SMOOTH AND CREAMY CONSISTENCY.
4. SQUEEZE IN THE JUICE OF ONE LIME FOR A REFRESHING CITRUS NOTE.
5. IF YOU LIKE YOUR SMOOTHIE COLD, ADD A FEW ICE CUBES TO THE BLENDER.
6. BLEND ON HIGH UNTIL SMOOTH AND CREAMY. IF THE SMOOTHIE IS TOO THICK, YOU CAN ADD A LITTLE WATER OR MORE COCONUT MILK TO REACH YOUR DESIRED CONSISTENCY.
7. POUR THE SMOOTHIE INTO GLASSES, GARNISHING WITH COCONUT FLAKES OR SHREDDED COCONUT IF DESIRED.

GREEN ZEN SMOOTHIE

INGREDIENTS

- 1 CUP SPINACH LEAVES, FRESH
- 1/2 CUP KALE LEAVES, STEMS REMOVED
- 1 MEDIUM RIPE AVOCADO, PEELED AND PITTED
- 1 RIPE BANANA, PEELED AND SLICED
- 1/2 CUP CUCUMBER, CHOPPED
- 1/2 CUP GREEN APPLE, CORED AND CHOPPED
- JUICE OF 1/2 LEMON
- A FEW MINT LEAVES, FOR A REFRESHING TWIST
- 1 CUP COLD WATER OR COCONUT WATER, FOR HYDRATION AND A HINT OF SWEETNESS
- OPTIONAL: 1 TABLESPOON CHIA SEEDS, FOR OMEGA-3S AND FIBER

DIRECTIONS

1. WASH THE SPINACH, KALE, AND MINT LEAVES THOROUGHLY.
2. IN A BLENDER, COMBINE THE SPINACH, KALE, AVOCADO, BANANA, CUCUMBER, GREEN APPLE, AND MINT LEAVES.
3. ADD THE LEMON JUICE AND COLD WATER OR COCONUT WATER TO THE MIX. THE LIQUID HELPS TO BLEND ALL THE INGREDIENTS SMOOTHLY AND ADDS AN EXTRA LAYER OF HYDRATION.
4. FOR AN ADDITIONAL HEALTH BOOST, SPRINKLE IN THE CHIA SEEDS.
5. BLEND ON HIGH UNTIL THE MIXTURE BECOMES SMOOTH AND CREAMY. IF THE SMOOTHIE IS TOO THICK, YOU CAN ADD MORE WATER OR COCONUT WATER TO ACHIEVE YOUR DESIRED CONSISTENCY.
6. TASTE AND ADJUST THE SWEETNESS OR TARTNESS BY ADDING MORE BANANA OR LEMON JUICE IF NEEDED.
7. SERVE THE SMOOTHIE IMMEDIATELY, GARNISHED WITH A FEW MINT LEAVES OR A SPRINKLE OF CHIA SEEDS ON TOP FOR AN ELEGANT FINISH.

CUCUMBER CLEANSE

- 2 LARGE CUCUMBERS
- 4 STALKS OF CELERY
- JUICE OF 2 LIMES

1. WASH CUCUMBERS. PEEL IF NOT ORGANIC FOR A SMOOTHER JUICE; OTHERWISE, KEEP THE SKIN FOR EXTRA NUTRIENTS.
2. CLEAN AND CHOP CELERY INTO JUICER-FRIENDLY SIZES.
3. EXTRACT JUICE FROM THE LIMES, ENSURING NO SEEDS GET IN.
4. START WITH JUICING CUCUMBERS, THEN ADD CELERY TO THE JUICER FOR A BLEND RICH IN HYDRATION AND NUTRIENTS.
5. MIX IN THE LIME JUICE FOR A TANGY KICK AND VITAMIN C BOOST.
6. STIR WELL AND SERVE THE JUICE IMMEDIATELY FOR ITS REFRESHING AND DETOXIFYING BENEFITS.

PEAR FENNEL FUSION

INGREDIENTS

- 2 RIPE PEARS, CORED AND SLICED
- 1 SMALL FENNEL BULB, TRIMMED AND CHOPPED
- 1 CUP SPINACH LEAVES

DIRECTIONS

1. SELECT RIPE PEARS FOR SWEETNESS, CORE AND SLICE.
2. PREPARE THE FENNEL BULB BY TRIMMING OFF FRONDS AND THE HARD BOTTOM, THEN CHOP.
3. THOROUGHLY WASH SPINACH LEAVES.
4. BEGIN JUICING WITH SPINACH, AS ITS LEAFY STRUCTURE JUICES WELL BETWEEN MORE SUBSTANTIAL ITEMS LIKE FENNEL AND PEARS.
5. CONTINUE WITH FENNEL, ADDING ITS DIGESTIVE BENEFITS, THEN FINISH WITH PEARS TO ENSURE A THOROUGH BLEND OF ALL FLAVORS.
6. STIR THE JUICE WELL BEFORE SERVING TO FULLY INTEGRATE THE DIVERSE TASTES.
7. ENJOY THE PEAR FENNEL FUSION FRESH FOR ITS MAXIMUM DIGESTIVE AID AND REFRESHMENT. IDEAL FOR A NOURISHING SNACK OR A GENTLE, DIGESTIVE-SUPPORTING DRINK.

SWEET POTATO SUNRISE

- 1 LARGE SWEET POTATO, PEELED AND CHOPPED
- 4 LARGE CARROTS, WASHED AND CHOPPED
- 1/2 TEASPOON GROUND CINNAMON

1. PREPARE THE SWEET POTATO BY PEELING AND CHOPPING IT INTO JUICER-FRIENDLY PIECES. SWEET POTATOES ARE RICH IN ESSENTIAL NUTRIENTS.
2. CHOP THE CARROTS AFTER WASHING THEM WELL. THEY CONTRIBUTE SWEETNESS AND A BOOST OF BETA-CAROTENE.
3. MEASURE THE GROUND CINNAMON, READY TO ADD ITS AROMATIC AND HEALTH-PROMOTING QUALITIES.
4. JUICE THE SWEET POTATO AND CARROTS TOGETHER, BLENDING THEIR FLAVORS AND NUTRITIONAL BENEFITS.
5. STIR IN THE CINNAMON AFTER JUICING FOR ADDED FLAVOR AND HEALTH PERKS.
6. SERVE THE SWEET POTATO SUNRISE IMMEDIATELY, SAVORING ITS NUTRITIOUS, COMFORTING QUALITIES. IDEAL FOR A MORNING ENERGIZER OR A SWEET AFTERNOON LIFT.

RADIANT GLOW ELIXIR

- 1 LARGE CUCUMBER
- 1/4 CUP ALOE VERA JUICE
- JUICE OF 1 LEMON
- A SMALL HANDFUL OF FRESH MINT LEAVES

1. WASH AND CHOP THE CUCUMBER. PEEL IF NOT ORGANIC TO REDUCE PESTICIDE INTAKE, ENHANCING THE DRINK'S SKIN-HYDRATING BENEFITS.
2. CONFIRM THE ALOE VERA JUICE IS INGESTIBLE AND MEASURE OUT 1/4 CUP, KNOWN FOR ITS SKIN-SOOTHING AND HYDRATING PROPERTIES.
3. EXTRACT JUICE FROM THE LEMON, ENSURING NO SEEDS REMAIN. LEMON'S VITAMIN C SUPPORTS SKIN BRIGHTNESS AND COLLAGEN FORMATION.
4. THOROUGHLY CLEAN THE MINT LEAVES, READY TO ADD THEIR REFRESHING AND SOOTHING FLAVOR.
5. FOR JUICING: JUICE THE CUCUMBER AND MINT FIRST, THEN STIR IN THE ALOE VERA AND LEMON JUICE.
6. FOR BLENDING: BLEND CUCUMBER AND MINT WITH A LITTLE WATER, STRAIN, THEN MIX IN THE ALOE VERA AND LEMON JUICE.
7. STIR ALL INGREDIENTS WELL, ENSURING A HARMONIOUS BLEND OF FLAVORS. SERVE CHILLED FOR A REFRESHING BEAUTY TONIC.
8. ENJOY THIS RADIANT GLOW ELIXIR TO HYDRATE AND REVITALIZE YOUR SKIN FROM THE INSIDE OUT, IDEAL FOR A MORNING REFRESH OR AN AFTERNOON HYDRATION BOOST.

SWEET ALMOND DREAM

INGREDIENTS

- 1 CUP ALMOND MILK
- 1 RIPE BANANA
- A DASH OF CINNAMON

DIRECTIONS

1. IN A BLENDER, COMBINE ALMOND MILK AND THE RIPE BANANA. THE ALMOND MILK ENRICHES THE DRINK WITH VITAMIN E AND HEALTHY FATS, WHILE THE BANANA BRINGS POTASSIUM AND SWEETNESS.
2. ADD A DASH OF CINNAMON FOR A TOUCH OF ANTI-INFLAMMATORY BENEFITS AND A WARM, COMFORTING FLAVOR.
3. BLEND UNTIL THE MIXTURE IS CREAMY AND SMOOTH.
4. SERVE THE SWEET ALMOND DREAM IMMEDIATELY, ENJOYING IT AS A DELICIOUSLY HYDRATING MORNING BEVERAGE OR A SOOTHING EVENING SNACK.

FAT FLUSH WATER

- 1 LARGE GRAPEFRUIT
- JUICE OF 1 LEMON
- A SMALL HANDFUL OF FRESH MINT LEAVES

1. PEEL AND SEGMENT THE GRAPEFRUIT, CAREFULLY REMOVING ANY SEEDS. GRAPEFRUIT BOOSTS FAT BURNING WITH ITS ENZYMES AND VITAMIN C.
2. EXTRACT JUICE FROM THE LEMON, ENSURING IT'S SEEDLESS. LEMON SUPPORTS DETOX AND DIGESTION.
3. WASH THE MINT LEAVES, WHICH ADD A REFRESHING FLAVOR AND AID DIGESTION.
4. FOR JUICING: JUICE GRAPEFRUIT AND MINT TOGETHER, THEN MIX IN LEMON JUICE.
5. FOR BLENDING: BLEND GRAPEFRUIT AND MINT WITH A SPLASH OF WATER, STRAIN, AND THEN STIR IN LEMON JUICE.
6. ENSURE ALL INGREDIENTS ARE WELL COMBINED. SERVE CHILLED FOR A REFRESHING AND METABOLISM-BOOSTING DRINK.

GREEN TEA ZEST

- 1 CUP BREWED GREEN TEA, COOLED
- 1 LARGE CUCUMBER
- A SMALL HANDFUL OF FRESH MINT LEAVES

1. BREW THE GREEN TEA AND LET IT COOL. THE CATECHINS IN GREEN TEA ARE GREAT FOR ENHANCING FAT BURN AND INCREASING METABOLISM.
2. CHOP THE CUCUMBER AND WASH THE MINT LEAVES.
3. IN A BLENDER, COMBINE THE COOLED GREEN TEA, CUCUMBER, AND MINT LEAVES. BLEND UNTIL THE MIXTURE IS SMOOTH.
4. SERVE THE GREEN TEA ZEST CHILLED FOR MAXIMUM REFRESHMENT.

APPLE CIDER VINEGAR TONIC

INGREDIENTS

- 2 TABLESPOONS APPLE CIDER VINEGAR (WITH "THE MOTHER")
- JUICE OF 1 LEMON
- 1 TEASPOON HONEY (OPTIONAL, FOR SWEETNESS)
- 1 CUP WATER

DIRECTIONS

1. IN A GLASS, COMBINE THE APPLE CIDER VINEGAR AND LEMON JUICE WITH WATER. THE APPLE CIDER VINEGAR OFFERS BENEFITS LIKE LOWERING BLOOD SUGAR LEVELS, AIDING DIGESTION, AND PROMOTING FAT BURN.
2. STIR IN HONEY TO SWEETEN, IF YOU LIKE, PROVIDING A SMOOTHER TASTE AND ADDITIONAL ANTIOXIDANT PROPERTIES.
3. ENJOY THIS TONIC IN THE MORNING TO BOOST YOUR METABOLISM OR BEFORE MEALS TO SUPPORT DIGESTION.

STRAWBERRY SUNRISE SMOOTHIE

INGREDIENTS

- 1 CUP FRESH STRAWBERRIES, HULLED
- 1/2 CUP PLAIN OR VANILLA YOGURT (FOR CREAMINESS AND PROBIOTICS)
- 1/2 BANANA, SLICED (FOR NATURAL SWEETNESS AND THICKNESS)
- 1/2 CUP ORANGE JUICE (FOR A CITRUSY KICK AND VITAMIN C)
- A DASH OF VANILLA EXTRACT (ENHANCES FLAVOR, OPTIONAL)
- ICE CUBES (OPTIONAL, FOR A COOLER DRINK)

DIRECTIONS

1. ADD STRAWBERRIES, YOGURT, BANANA, AND ORANGE JUICE INTO A BLENDER. INCLUDE A DASH OF VANILLA EXTRACT FOR AN EXTRA FLAVOR BOOST.
2. BLEND UNTIL SMOOTH. IF THE MIXTURE IS TOO THICK, YOU CAN ADD A LITTLE MORE ORANGE JUICE OR WATER TO ADJUST THE CONSISTENCY.
3. ADD ICE CUBES IF YOU PREFER YOUR SMOOTHIE CHILLED, BLENDING UNTIL SMOOTH.
4. SERVE THE STRAWBERRY SUNRISE SMOOTHIE IMMEDIATELY, GARNISHED WITH A STRAWBERRY OR A SLICE OF ORANGE ON THE RIM OF THE GLASS FOR A FESTIVE LOOK.

PEACHY KEEN COOLER

INGREDIENTS

- 2 RIPE PEACHES, PITTED AND SLICED
- 1/2 TEASPOON FRESHLY GRATED GINGER (FOR A SPICY NOTE AND DIGESTIVE AID)
- 1 TABLESPOON HONEY (ADJUST TO TASTE, OPTIONAL FOR EXTRA SWEETNESS)
- JUICE OF 1 LIME (FOR TARTNESS AND FRESHNESS)
- 1 CUP SPARKLING WATER (FOR A FIZZY LIFT)
- ICE CUBES

DIRECTIONS

1. IN A BLENDER, COMBINE PEACHES, GRATED GINGER, HONEY, AND LIME JUICE. BLEND UNTIL SMOOTH.
2. STRAIN THE MIXTURE THROUGH A FINE SIEVE INTO A PITCHER TO REMOVE THE PULP, IF DESIRED, FOR A SMOOTHER DRINK.
3. ADD ICE CUBES TO GLASSES, AND POUR THE PEACH MIXTURE OVER THEM, FILLING ABOUT HALFWAY.
4. TOP OFF EACH GLASS WITH SPARKLING WATER, GENTLY STIR TO COMBINE.
5. GARNISH WITH A PEACH SLICE OR A LIME WHEEL, AND SERVE THE PEACHY KEEN COOLER IMMEDIATELY FOR A BURST OF COOL, REFRESHING FLAVOR.

OMEGA BOOST

- 1 CUP SPINACH LEAVES
- 2 STALKS OF CELERY
- 1 LARGE CUCUMBER
- 1 TABLESPOON FLAXSEED OIL

1. WASH THE SPINACH, CELERY, AND CUCUMBER THOROUGHLY. CHOP CELERY AND CUCUMBER INTO PIECES THAT FIT YOUR JUICER. KEEP THE CUCUMBER SKIN IF ORGANIC FOR ADDED NUTRIENTS.
2. JUICE THE SPINACH, CELERY, AND CUCUMBER TOGETHER TO CREATE A HYDRATING, VITAMIN-RICH BASE.
3. STIR FLAXSEED OIL INTO THE FRESHLY MADE JUICE. THE FLAXSEED OIL ENRICHES THE DRINK WITH OMEGA-3 FATTY ACIDS, BENEFICIAL FOR REDUCING INFLAMMATION AND PROMOTING HEART HEALTH.
4. MIX WELL TO ENSURE THE OIL IS FULLY INCORPORATED. SERVE THE OMEGA BOOST IMMEDIATELY, TAKING ADVANTAGE OF ITS FRESH, NOURISHING QUALITIES.

POMEGRANATE PASSION

- 1 CUP POMEGRANATE SEEDS
- JUICE OF 1 ORANGE
- JUICE OF 1/2 LEMON

1. USE A JUICER TO EXTRACT JUICE FROM THE POMEGRANATE SEEDS. IF YOU DON'T HAVE A JUICER, MANUALLY PRESS THE SEEDS OVER A STRAINER TO COLLECT THE JUICE.
2. SQUEEZE THE JUICE OF ONE ORANGE AND HALF A LEMON, ENSURING NO SEEDS FALL INTO THE MIX.
3. COMBINE THE POMEGRANATE, ORANGE, AND LEMON JUICES IN A GLASS, STIRRING WELL TO MIX THE VIBRANT FLAVORS AND NUTRIENTS.
4. SERVE THE POMEGRANATE PASSION IMMEDIATELY TO CAPTURE THE ESSENCE OF ITS FRESH, ANTIOXIDANT-RICH BENEFITS.

CITRUS OMEGA WAVE

- 2 LARGE ORANGES, PEELED
- 3 LARGE CARROTS, WASHED AND CHOPPED
- 1 TABLESPOON FLAXSEED OIL

1. BEGIN BY JUICING THE PEELED ORANGES AND CHOPPED CARROTS. THIS MIX BRINGS TOGETHER THE IMMUNE-BOOSTING VITAMIN C FROM ORANGES WITH THE VISION-SUPPORTING BETA-CAROTENE FROM CARROTS, PROMOTING HEART HEALTH AND OVERALL WELLNESS.
2. AFTER JUICING THE FRUITS AND VEGETABLES, STIR IN THE FLAXSEED OIL TO THE JUICE. THE FLAXSEED OIL IS NOT ONLY A GREAT SOURCE OF ALA (ALPHA-LINOLENIC ACID), AN ESSENTIAL OMEGA-3 FATTY ACID THAT SUPPORTS HEART HEALTH, BUT IT ALSO ADDS A DISTINCT NUTTY FLAVOR THAT ENHANCES THE NATURAL SWEETNESS OF THE JUICE.
3. MAKE SURE THE JUICE AND OIL ARE THOROUGHLY MIXED. SERVE THE CITRUS OMEGA WAVE RIGHT AWAY TO SAVOR ITS FRESH, ENERGETIC FLAVORS AND HEALTH BENEFITS. THIS BEVERAGE IS PERFECT FOR A NUTRITIOUS START TO THE DAY OR AS A REVITALIZING MIDDAY REFRESHMENT.

TOMATO TANGO

- 3 LARGE TOMATOES
- 1 RED PEPPER, DESEEDED
- 1 CLOVE OF GARLIC, PEELED
- A PINCH OF CAYENNE PEPPER

1. BEGIN BY WASHING AND QUARTERING THE TOMATOES. TOMATOES ARE NOT JUST DELICIOUS; THEY'RE ALSO A GREAT SOURCE OF LYCOPENE, AN ANTIOXIDANT KNOWN FOR ITS HEART HEALTH BENEFITS.
2. PREPARE THE RED PEPPER BY WASHING, DESEEDING, AND CHOPPING IT. PACKED WITH VITAMINS A AND C, RED PEPPERS ARE EXCELLENT FOR BOOSTING HEART HEALTH AND IMMUNITY.
3. PEEL THE GARLIC CLOVE. GARLIC IS CELEBRATED FOR ITS ALLICIN CONTENT, WHICH HAS BEEN SHOWN TO IMPROVE HEART HEALTH BY LOWERING BLOOD PRESSURE AND CHOLESTEROL LEVELS.
4. JUICE THE TOMATOES, RED PEPPER, AND GARLIC TOGETHER. IF YOUR JUICER STRUGGLES WITH SOFTER TEXTURES OR FIBROUS MATERIALS, CONSIDER BLENDING AND THEN STRAINING THE MIXTURE FOR A SMOOTHER JUICE.
5. STIR A PINCH OF CAYENNE PEPPER INTO THE JUICE ACCORDING TO YOUR TASTE PREFERENCE. CAYENNE PEPPER NOT ONLY ADDS A SPICY DEPTH TO THE JUICE BUT ALSO AIDS IN METABOLISM AND CIRCULATION.
6. ENSURE ALL INGREDIENTS ARE THOROUGHLY MIXED AND SERVE THE TOMATO TANGO IMMEDIATELY. THIS JUICE IS AN IDEAL CHOICE FOR A HEALTHFUL START TO THE DAY OR A REFRESHING PICK-ME-UP IN THE AFTERNOON, OFFERING A SAVORY TWIST ON TRADITIONAL FRUIT JUICES WHILE PACKING A PUNCH OF BENEFICIAL NUTRIENTS FOR THE HEART.

ALMOND BLISS

- 1 CUP ALMOND MILK
- 1 CUP FRESH SPINACH LEAVES
- 1 CUP BLUEBERRIES (FRESH OR FROZEN)

1. START BY ADDING THE ALMOND MILK TO A BLENDER. ALMOND MILK IS NOT ONLY A CREAMY BASE BUT ALSO A SOURCE OF VITAMIN E, WHICH BENEFITS HEART HEALTH.
2. ADD THE FRESH SPINACH LEAVES. SPINACH IS PACKED WITH FIBER, VITAMINS, AND MINERALS, ALL CONTRIBUTING TO A STRONG, HEALTHY HEART.
3. INCORPORATE THE BLUEBERRIES. WHETHER YOU OPT FOR FRESH OR FROZEN, BLUEBERRIES ADD A SWEET, TANGY FLAVOR AND ARE LOADED WITH ANTIOXIDANTS THAT FIGHT OXIDATIVE STRESS AND INFLAMMATION.
4. BLEND ALL THE INGREDIENTS TOGETHER UNTIL THE MIXTURE IS COMPLETELY SMOOTH. IF YOU'RE USING FROZEN BLUEBERRIES, YOUR ALMOND BLISS WILL HAVE A NATURALLY CHILLED AND REFRESHING TEXTURE.
5. ONCE SMOOTH, POUR YOUR ALMOND BLISS INTO A GLASS AND ENJOY IT IMMEDIATELY. THIS SMOOTHIE IS IDEAL FOR ANYONE LOOKING FOR A QUICK, HEALTHFUL BREAKFAST, A REJUVENATING SNACK, OR A SATISFYING POST-EXERCISE DRINK. ITS BLEND OF INGREDIENTS NOT ONLY SUPPORTS HEART HEALTH BUT ALSO ENERGIZES AND DELIGHTS THE TASTE BUDS.

CLARITY COOLER

INGREDIENTS

- 1 CUP BLUEBERRIES (FRESH OR FROZEN)
- 2 CUPS SPINACH LEAVES
- 1 TABLESPOON FLAXSEED OIL
- JUICE OF 1 ORANGE

DIRECTIONS

1. RINSE FRESH BLUEBERRIES OR USE FROZEN DIRECTLY FOR A CHILLED EFFECT. CLEAN SPINACH LEAVES WELL.
2. JUICE THE ORANGE AND ADJUST THE AMOUNT FOR YOUR PREFERRED TANGINESS.
3. IN A BLENDER, MIX THE BLUEBERRIES, SPINACH, AND ORANGE JUICE UNTIL SMOOTH.
4. STIR IN FLAXSEED OIL, BLENDING ITS OMEGA-3 BENEFITS WITHOUT ALTERING TASTE.
5. SERVE THE CLARITY COOLER FRESH FOR OPTIMAL FLAVOR AND NUTRIENT INTAKE.

SUNSHINE LIFT

- 1 RIPE MANGO, PEELED AND CUBED
- JUICE OF 2 ORANGES
- 1 RIPE BANANA

1. PEEL AND CUBE THE MANGO; SQUEEZE THE JUICE FROM 2 ORANGES; PEEL THE BANANA.
2. PLACE MANGO, ORANGE JUICE, AND BANANA IN A BLENDER.
3. BLEND UNTIL SMOOTH.
4. POUR INTO A GLASS AND ENJOY IMMEDIATELY FOR AN UPLIFTING TROPICAL TREAT.

FOCUS FUEL

INGREDIENTS

- 1 CUP BLACKBERRIES
- 1 MEDIUM BEETROOT, PEELED AND CHOPPED
- 2 LARGE APPLES, CORED AND SLICED
- 1/4 TEASPOON GREEN COFFEE BEAN EXTRACT

DIRECTIONS

1. JUICE BLACKBERRIES, BEETROOT, AND APPLES. THIS MIX BRINGS TOGETHER ANTIOXIDANTS FROM BLACKBERRIES, COGNITIVE-ENHANCING NITRATES FROM BEETROOT, AND FIBER AND NATURAL SWEETNESS FROM APPLES.
2. STIR IN THE GREEN COFFEE BEAN EXTRACT TO THE FRESHLY MADE JUICE. THIS INGREDIENT ADDS A BOOST OF NATURAL CAFFEINE AND CHLOROGENIC ACIDS, AIDING IN FOCUS AND METABOLISM.
3. MIX THOROUGHLY TO ENSURE THE GREEN COFFEE BEAN EXTRACT IS WELL INTEGRATED. SERVE THE FOCUS FUEL FRESH FOR AN IMMEDIATE BOOST IN CONCENTRATION AND ENERGY.

MEMORY MAGIC

- 1 CUP PUMPKIN SEED MILK (HOMEMADE OR STORE-BOUGHT)
- 1 CUP STRAWBERRIES, HULLED
- 1 SPRIG OF ROSEMARY

1. PREPARE THE PUMPKIN SEED MILK BY BLENDING SOAKED PUMPKIN SEEDS WITH WATER UNTIL SMOOTH, THEN STRAIN. PUMPKIN SEEDS ARE RICH IN ZINC, SUPPORTING BRAIN HEALTH AND MEMORY.
2. JUICE STRAWBERRIES ALONG WITH A SPRIG OF ROSEMARY. STRAWBERRIES BRING ANTIOXIDANTS TO DEFEND AGAINST OXIDATIVE STRESS, WHILE ROSEMARY CAN ENHANCE COGNITIVE FUNCTION.
3. COMBINE THE STRAWBERRY AND ROSEMARY JUICE WITH PUMPKIN SEED MILK, MIXING WELL TO BLEND THE FLAVORS.
4. SERVE THE MEMORY MAGIC FRESH, ENJOYING THE SYNERGISTIC EFFECTS OF ITS INGREDIENTS ON BRAIN HEALTH AND COGNITIVE FUNCTION, IDEAL FOR A MORNING BOOST OR A MENTAL LIFT ANY TIME OF THE DAY.

HAPPY BERRY

INGREDIENTS

- 1 CUP AÇAI BERRY JUICE
- 1 CUP RASPBERRIES (FRESH OR FROZEN)
- 1 TABLESPOON DARK CHOCOLATE (COCOA POWDER), UNSWEETENED

DIRECTIONS

1. IN A BLENDER, MIX THE AÇAI BERRY JUICE WITH RASPBERRIES. AÇAI BERRIES BRING ANTIOXIDANTS AND MOOD-SUPPORTIVE OMEGA-3 FATTY ACIDS, WHILE RASPBERRIES OFFER A TANGY TASTE PLUS EXTRA FIBER AND VITAMINS.
2. ADD THE UNSWEETENED COCOA POWDER. COCOA BOOSTS ENDORPHIN PRODUCTION FOR A HAPPY SENSATION AND SUPPORTS BRAIN HEALTH WITH FLAVONOIDS.
3. BLEND UNTIL SMOOTH, ADDING A BIT OF WATER OR MORE AÇAI JUICE IF NEEDED FOR A PREFERRED CONSISTENCY.
4. SERVE THE HAPPY BERRY FRESH FOR AN INSTANT MOOD LIFT, WHETHER AS A JOYFUL BEGINNING TO YOUR DAY OR A SATISFYING, HEALTHY DESSERT.

OMEGA MIND

- 1 CUP WALNUT MILK (HOMEMADE OR STORE-BOUGHT)
- 2 KIWIS, PEELED AND SLICED
- 2 CUPS KALE LEAVES, STEMS REMOVED

1. PREPARE WALNUT MILK BY BLENDING SOAKED WALNUTS WITH WATER UNTIL SMOOTH, THEN STRAINING. WALNUT MILK CONTRIBUTES OMEGA-3 FATTY ACIDS, SUPPORTING BRAIN HEALTH AND COGNITIVE FUNCTION.
2. JUICE THE SLICED KIWIS AND STEMLESS KALE LEAVES. KIWIS OFFER VITAMIN C AND ANTIOXIDANTS FOR BRAIN PROTECTION, WHILE KALE PROVIDES ADDITIONAL NUTRIENTS AND ANTIOXIDANTS.
3. COMBINE THE KIWI AND KALE JUICE WITH WALNUT MILK, MIXING WELL TO ENSURE A SMOOTH CONSISTENCY.
4. SERVE THE OMEGA MIND FRESH, ENJOYING THE BLEND OF FLAVORS AND THE BOOST IT PROVIDES TO YOUR MENTAL WELL-BEING.

MOOD MENDER

INGREDIENTS

- 1 RIPE AVOCADO
- 2 LARGE CARROTS, CHOPPED
- JUICE OF 2 ORANGES
- 1 INCH GINGER ROOT, PEELED

DIRECTIONS

1. HALVE AND SCOOP OUT THE AVOCADO. CHOP CARROTS FOR JUICING. JUICE THE ORANGES AND PEEL AND SLICE THE GINGER.
2. JUICE CARROTS AND GINGER TOGETHER.
3. BLEND THE AVOCADO FLESH WITH THE CARROT-GINGER JUICE AND ORANGE JUICE UNTIL CREAMY.
4. SERVE IMMEDIATELY FOR AN UPLIFTING TREAT PACKED WITH MOOD-ENHANCING NUTRIENTS.

SPRING AWAKENING

INGREDIENTS

- 2 CUPS SPRING GREENS (LIKE SPINACH, KALE, OR MIXED YOUNG GREENS)
- 1 LARGE CUCUMBER
- A SMALL HANDFUL OF FRESH MINT LEAVES
- JUICE OF 1 LEMON

DIRECTIONS

1. RINSE THE SPRING GREENS TO ELIMINATE DIRT, ENRICHING YOUR DRINK WITH THEIR DETOXIFYING VITAMINS AND CHLOROPHYLL.
2. WASH AND CHOP THE CUCUMBER; KEEP THE SKIN IF IT'S ORGANIC FOR ADDED NUTRIENTS. CUCUMBERS BOOST HYDRATION AND OVERALL HEALTH.
3. CLEAN THE MINT LEAVES, ADDING A BURST OF REFRESHING FLAVOR KNOWN FOR AIDING DIGESTION.
4. SQUEEZE THE LEMON FOR A ZEST THAT COMPLEMENTS THE GREENS AND AIDS IN NUTRIENT ABSORPTION.
5. IF JUICING, PRESS MINT AND GREENS FIRST, THEN CUCUMBER, MIXING IN LEMON JUICE LAST FOR A VIBRANT BLEND OF FLAVORS AND NUTRIENTS.
6. FOR BLENDING, COMBINE ALL INGREDIENTS WITH A SPLASH OF WATER UNTIL SMOOTH, STRAINING FOR SILKINESS IF PREFERRED.
7. SERVE THE SPRING AWAKENING CHILLED, SAVORING THIS ENERGIZING DRINK AS A DELIGHTFUL MORNING START OR A REJUVENATING DAYTIME REFRESHMENT.

ALMOND CHOCOLATE BLISS

INGREDIENTS

- 1 CUP ALMOND MILK
- 1 RIPE BANANA
- 2 TABLESPOONS UNSWEETENED COCOA POWDER
- 1 TABLESPOON ALMOND BUTTER
- 1 TABLESPOON HONEY (OR TO TASTE)

DIRECTIONS

1. INTO YOUR BLENDER, ADD 1 CUP OF ALMOND MILK, 1 SLICED RIPE BANANA, 2 TABLESPOONS OF UNSWEETENED COCOA POWDER, AND 1 TABLESPOON OF ALMOND BUTTER.
2. ADD 1 TABLESPOON OF HONEY TO THE BLENDER, ADJUSTING THE AMOUNT ACCORDING TO YOUR TASTE PREFERENCE FOR SWEETNESS.
3. BLEND EVERYTHING ON HIGH UNTIL THE MIXTURE BECOMES SMOOTH AND CREAMY. IF IT SEEMS TOO THICK, YOU CAN THIN IT OUT BY ADDING A BIT MORE ALMOND MILK.
4. AFTER BLENDING, TASTE THE SMOOTHIE AND DECIDE IF YOU'D LIKE IT SWEETER OR MORE CHOCOLATY, THEN ADJUST BY ADDING MORE HONEY OR COCOA POWDER AS NEEDED.
5. POUR THE SMOOTHIE INTO A GLASS, OPTIONALLY GARNISH WITH A SPRINKLE OF COCOA POWDER OR SOME SLICED ALMONDS, AND ENJOY RIGHT AWAY.

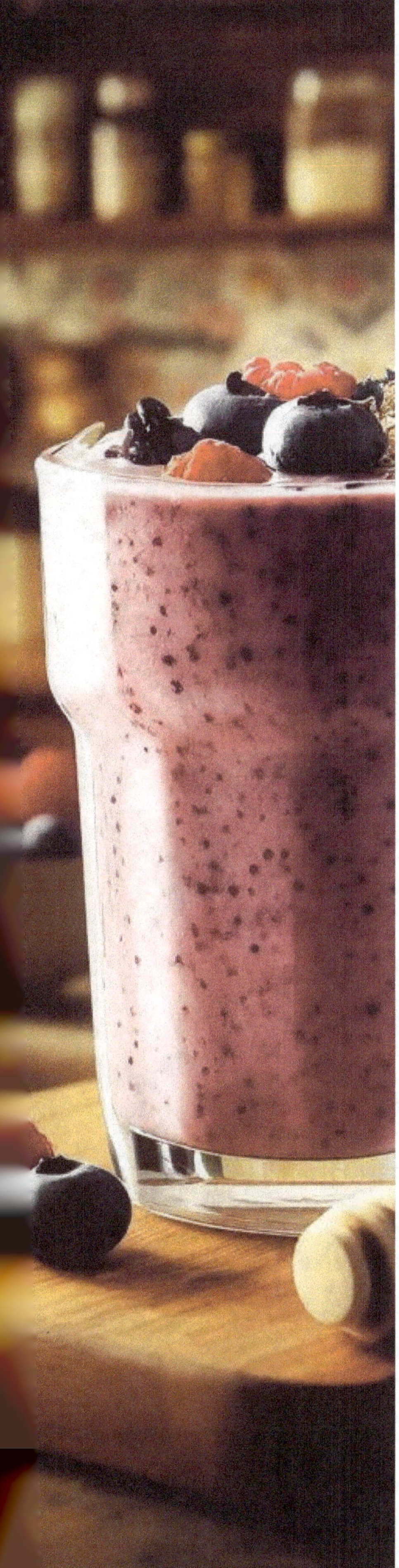

BERRY SOY DELIGHT

- A GENEROUS CUP OF MIXED BERRIES (FRESH OR FROZEN)
- 1 CUP OF SOY MILK
- 1 SCOOP OF VANILLA PROTEIN POWDER
- HONEY, TO TASTE

1. ADD THE MIXED BERRIES AND SOY MILK TO A BLENDER. THE BERRIES OFFER VIBRANT FLAVORS AND ANTIOXIDANTS, WHILE SOY MILK PROVIDES A CREAMY, PROTEIN-RICH BASE.
2. INCORPORATE A SCOOP OF VANILLA PROTEIN POWDER, ENHANCING THE SMOOTHIE'S PROTEIN CONTENT AND ADDING A HINT OF VANILLA FLAVOR.
3. DRIZZLE HONEY OVER THE OTHER INGREDIENTS, SWEETENING THE SMOOTHIE NATURALLY. ADJUST THE AMOUNT OF HONEY BASED ON HOW SWEET YOU LIKE YOUR SMOOTHIE.
4. BLEND ALL THE INGREDIENTS UNTIL THE MIXTURE IS SMOOTH. IF USING FROZEN BERRIES, YOU'LL END UP WITH A THICK, ALMOST MILKSHAKE-LIKE TEXTURE. IF THE SMOOTHIE IS TOO THICK, SIMPLY ADD A BIT MORE SOY MILK TO THIN IT OUT TO YOUR LIKING.
5. ONCE THOROUGHLY BLENDED AND SMOOTH, POUR THE BERRY SOY DELIGHT INTO A GLASS.

PEANUT BUTTER BANANA BOOST

INGREDIENTS

- 1 RIPE BANANA
- 2 TABLESPOONS SMOOTH PEANUT BUTTER
- 1 CUP ALMOND MILK
- 1 TABLESPOON COCOA POWDER

DIRECTIONS

1. PEEL THE BANANA AND ADD IT TO A BLENDER.
2. INCORPORATE THE SMOOTH PEANUT BUTTER, ENSURING IT'S WELL-MEASURED FOR A RICH, NUTTY FLAVOR.
3. POUR IN THE ALMOND MILK, PROVIDING A CREAMY LIQUID BASE FOR THE SMOOTHIE.
4. ADD A TABLESPOON OF COCOA POWDER TO INTRODUCE A SUBTLE CHOCOLATEY HINT THAT COMPLEMENTS THE PEANUT BUTTER AND BANANA FLAVORS.
5. BLEND ALL THE INGREDIENTS UNTIL SMOOTH. IF THE MIXTURE IS TOO THICK, YOU CAN ADJUST BY ADDING A LITTLE MORE ALMOND MILK.
6. ONCE ACHIEVED A SMOOTH CONSISTENCY, POUR THE PEANUT BUTTER BANANA BOOST INTO A GLASS AND ENJOY IMMEDIATELY FOR AN ENERGY-PACKED TREAT.

AVOCADO DREAM

- 1 RIPE AVOCADO
- 1 RIPE BANANA
- 1 CUP FRESH SPINACH LEAVES
- 1 CUP ALMOND MILK
- HONEY, TO TASTE

1. HALVE THE AVOCADO, REMOVE THE PIT, AND SCOOP THE FLESH INTO A BLENDER.
2. ADD THE PEELED RIPE BANANA TO THE BLENDER FOR NATURAL SWEETNESS.
3. WASH THE SPINACH LEAVES AND ADD THEM TO THE MIX, BRINGING IN A WEALTH OF VITAMINS AND MINERALS.
4. POUR IN THE ALMOND MILK TO CREATE A SMOOTH, LIQUID BASE.
5. SWEETEN WITH HONEY ACCORDING TO YOUR PREFERENCE, BALANCING THE FLAVORS OF THE SMOOTHIE.
6. BLEND UNTIL THE MIXTURE IS COMPLETELY SMOOTH. ADD MORE ALMOND MILK IF NEEDED TO REACH YOUR DESIRED CONSISTENCY.
7. SERVE THE AVOCADO DREAM SMOOTHIE IN A GLASS, READY TO SIP ON THIS NUTRITIOUS AND DELICIOUS BLEND

GINGER PEACH POWER

- SLICED PEACHES (1 CUP OR ABOUT 2 MEDIUM PEACHES)
- 1 INCH OF GINGER ROOT, PEELED AND FINELY GRATED
- 1/2 CUP GREEK YOGURT
- HONEY, TO TASTE (ABOUT 1 TABLESPOON)
- A SPLASH OF ALMOND MILK (ABOUT 1/4 CUP)

1. ADD THE SLICED PEACHES TO A BLENDER. IF PEACHES ARE NOT IN SEASON, FROZEN CAN BE A GREAT ALTERNATIVE.
2. GRATE THE GINGER ROOT DIRECTLY INTO THE BLENDER TO CAPTURE ITS SPICY, AROMATIC ESSENCE.
3. INCORPORATE THE GREEK YOGURT, PROVIDING A RICH, CREAMY TEXTURE AND A BOOST OF PROTEIN.
4. DRIZZLE IN HONEY FOR A NATURAL SWEETNESS THAT COMPLEMENTS THE PEACHES AND GINGER.
5. ADD A SPLASH OF ALMOND MILK TO ADJUST THE SMOOTHIE'S CONSISTENCY TO YOUR LIKING.
6. BLEND UNTIL SMOOTH, ENSURING THE GINGER IS WELL DISTRIBUTED THROUGHOUT THE SMOOTHIE.
7. TASTE AND ADJUST THE SWEETNESS, IF NECESSARY, BY ADDING MORE HONEY. SERVE THE GINGER PEACH POWER IMMEDIATELY, ENJOYING ITS REFRESHING AND ENERGIZING BLEND.

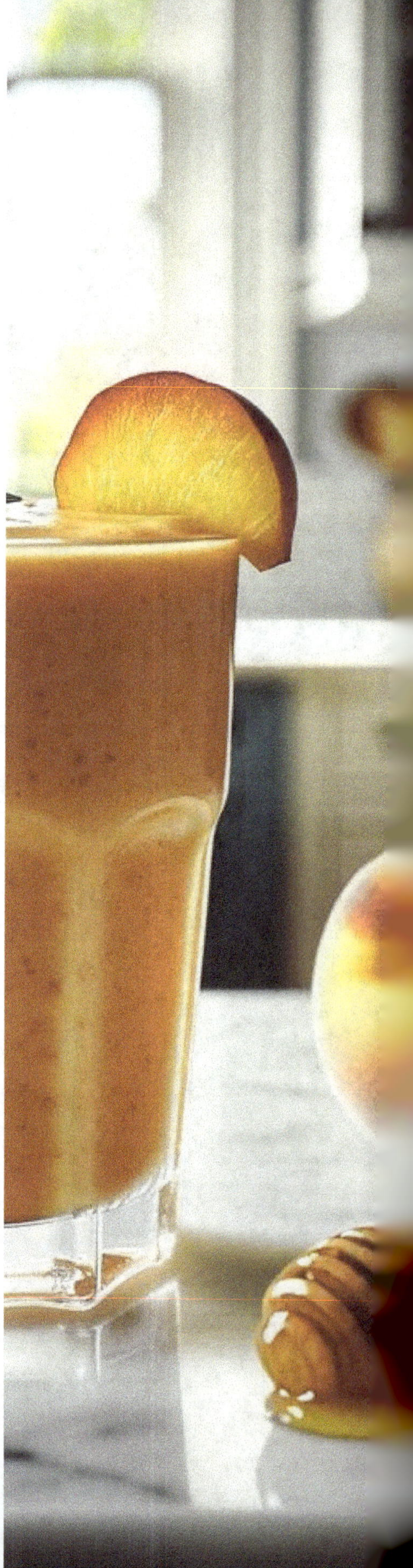

SUPERFOOD CHOCOLATE SMOOTHIE

- 1 CUP SPINACH LEAVES
- 1/2 RIPE AVOCADO
- 1 RIPE BANANA
- 2 TABLESPOONS RAW COCOA POWDER
- 1 TABLESPOON CHIA SEEDS
- 1 CUP COCONUT MILK

1. START BY ADDING FRESH SPINACH LEAVES TO THE BLENDER, PACKING A PUNCH OF VITAMINS AND MINERALS.
2. ADD THE AVOCADO AND BANANA FOR CREAMINESS AND NATURAL SWEETNESS.
3. SPRINKLE IN THE RAW COCOA POWDER FOR A DEEP, CHOCOLATY FLAVOR.
4. ADD CHIA SEEDS FOR THEIR OMEGA-3 FATTY ACIDS, FIBER, AND PROTEIN CONTENT.
5. POUR IN COCONUT MILK, ENHANCING THE SMOOTHIE'S TROPICAL FLAVOR AND CREAMY TEXTURE.
6. BLEND ALL THE INGREDIENTS UNTIL THE SMOOTHIE IS CREAMY AND SMOOTH, MAKING SURE THERE ARE NO SPINACH LEAF BITS LEFT UNBLENDED.
7. SERVE THE SUPERFOOD CHOCOLATE SMOOTHIE IMMEDIATELY, DIVING INTO A DECADENT YET HEALTHY CHOCOLATY TREAT THAT'S PERFECT FOR ANY TIME OF THE DAY.

BROCCOLI ORCHARD DELIGHT

INGREDIENTS

- 1 CUP BROCCOLI FLORETS, WASHED
- 2 MEDIUM APPLES, CORED AND SLICED
- 1 PEAR, CORED AND SLICED
- JUICE OF 1/2 LEMON

DIRECTIONS

1. BEGIN BY WASHING THE BROCCOLI FLORETS THOROUGHLY TO REMOVE ANY IMPURITIES. BROCCOLI IS PACKED WITH VITAMINS, MINERALS, AND ANTIOXIDANTS THAT CAN ENHANCE THE NUTRITIONAL PROFILE OF YOUR JUICE.
2. CORE AND SLICE THE APPLES AND PEAR, CHOOSING RIPE FRUITS FOR A NATURAL SWEETNESS THAT WILL BALANCE THE TASTE OF THE BROCCOLI.
3. JUICE THE BROCCOLI, APPLES, AND PEAR TOGETHER, ALLOWING THEIR FLAVORS TO BLEND. THE APPLES AND PEAR ADD A FRUITY SWEETNESS THAT COMPLEMENTS THE EARTHINESS OF THE BROCCOLI.
4. AFTER JUICING, STIR IN THE JUICE OF HALF A LEMON. THE LEMON NOT ONLY ADDS A REFRESHING CITRUS NOTE BUT ALSO HELPS PRESERVE THE BRIGHT COLOR OF THE JUICE AND BOOSTS ITS VITAMIN C CONTENT.
5. MIX THE JUICE WELL TO ENSURE ALL THE FLAVORS ARE EVENLY DISTRIBUTED.
6. SERVE THE BROCCOLI ORCHARD DELIGHT IMMEDIATELY TO ENJOY ITS MAXIMUM FRESHNESS AND HEALTH BENEFITS. THIS JUICE IS PERFECT FOR AN INVIGORATING START TO THE DAY OR AS A NOURISHING MIDDAY SNACK.

GRAPE & GINGER GLOW

- 2 CUPS RED GRAPES, WASHED
- 1/2 INCH PIECE OF FRESH GINGER ROOT, PEELED
- 1 SMALL CUCUMBER, WASHED AND SLICED
- JUICE OF 1 LIME

DIRECTIONS

1. ENSURE THE RED GRAPES ARE THOROUGHLY WASHED TO REMOVE ANY PESTICIDES OR DIRT. RED GRAPES ARE NOT ONLY DELICIOUS BUT ARE ALSO RICH IN ANTIOXIDANTS, INCLUDING RESVERATROL, WHICH IS KNOWN FOR ITS HEART-HEALTH BENEFITS.
2. PEEL AND SLICE A SMALL PIECE OF GINGER ROOT. GINGER ADDS A WARMING SPICE TO THE JUICE AND HAS ANTI-INFLAMMATORY PROPERTIES.
3. WASH AND SLICE THE CUCUMBER. CUCUMBERS ADD HYDRATION TO THE JUICE, MAKING IT MORE REFRESHING, AND CONTAIN SEVERAL VITAMINS AND MINERALS.
4. START JUICING THE GRAPES, GINGER, AND CUCUMBER TOGETHER. THE SWEETNESS OF THE GRAPES BALANCES THE SPICINESS OF THE GINGER AND THE MILD FLAVOR OF THE CUCUMBER BEAUTIFULLY.
5. ONCE EVERYTHING IS JUICED, STIR IN THE FRESHLY SQUEEZED LIME JUICE. LIME ADDS A CITRUSY ZEST, ENHANCING THE FLAVOR AND ADDING A BOOST OF VITAMIN C.
6. MIX THE JUICE WELL TO ENSURE THAT ALL THE FLAVORS MELD TOGETHER SEAMLESSLY.
7. SERVE THE GRAPE & GINGER GLOW IMMEDIATELY, ENJOYING THE UNIQUE COMBINATION OF FLAVORS AND THE HEALTH BENEFITS IT OFFERS. THIS JUICE IS EXCELLENT FOR AN ENERGY BOOST, SUPPORTING HEART HEALTH, AND PROVIDING A REFRESHING HYDRATION SOURCE.

KIWI CITRUS PEAR PUNCH

- 2 KIWIS, PEELED AND SLICED
- JUICE OF 1 LEMON
- 1 PEAR, CORED AND SLICED

1. START BY PEELING AND SLICING THE KIWIS AND PEAR.
2. EITHER JUICE OR BLEND THE SLICED KIWIS AND PEAR. IF BLENDING, AIM FOR A SMOOTH TEXTURE AND THEN STRAIN TO REMOVE ANY PULP.
3. MIX IN THE FRESHLY SQUEEZED LEMON JUICE WITH THE KIWI AND PEAR JUICE.
4. IMMEDIATELY SERVE THE JUICE TO ENJOY ITS FRESH, VIBRANT TASTE.

PAPAYA SUNRISE JUICE

- 2 CUPS PAPAYA, CUBED
- JUICE OF 1 ORANGE
- 1 CARROT, CHOPPED
- 1/2 INCH GINGER, PEELED
- JUICE OF 1/2 LIME

1. PREPARE THE PAPAYA BY PEELING, SEEDING, AND CUBING IT.
2. JUICE ONE ORANGE FOR ITS SWEET CITRUS FLAVOR.
3. WASH AND CHOP THE CARROT.
4. PEEL AND SLICE THE GINGER FOR A SPICY NOTE.
5. SQUEEZE THE JUICE FROM HALF A LIME FOR A TANGY ZEST.
6. JUICE OR BLEND THE PAPAYA, ORANGE JUICE, CARROT, AND GINGER. IF BLENDING, ADD A LITTLE WATER AND THEN STRAIN.
7. STIR IN THE LIME JUICE WITH THE PREPARED JUICE.
8. SERVE IMMEDIATELY, ENJOYING THE REFRESHING AND NUTRIENT-RICH PAPAYA SUNRISE JUICE.

MELON MINT REFRESHER

INGREDIENTS

- 2 CUPS WATERMELON, CUBED
- 1 CUP HONEYDEW MELON, CUBED
- A SMALL HANDFUL OF FRESH MINT LEAVES
- JUICE OF 1 LIME

DIRECTIONS

1. CUBE THE WATERMELON AND HONEYDEW MELON AFTER REMOVING THE RIND.
2. RINSE THE MINT LEAVES THOROUGHLY.
3. SQUEEZE THE JUICE FROM ONE LIME.
4. IN A BLENDER, COMBINE THE WATERMELON, HONEYDEW MELON, MINT LEAVES, AND LIME JUICE. ADD A SPLASH OF WATER IF NEEDED TO HELP THE BLENDING PROCESS.
5. BLEND UNTIL SMOOTH. FOR A JUICE-LIKE CONSISTENCY, YOU CAN STRAIN THE MIXTURE TO REMOVE THE PULP, OR LEAVE AS IS FOR A THICKER SMOOTHIE-STYLE DRINK.
6. SERVE THE MELON MINT REFRESHER CHILLED FOR A BURST OF HYDRATION AND FRESHNESS.

MILK PINEAPPLE STRAWBERRY BLISS

- 1 CUP COCONUT MILK
- 1 CUP PINEAPPLE, CUBED
- 1 CUP STRAWBERRIES, HULLED
- ICE CUBES (OPTIONAL)

1. POUR 1 CUP OF COCONUT MILK INTO A BLENDER. THIS ADDS A TROPICAL CREAMINESS.
2. ADD CUBED PINEAPPLE FOR ITS TANGY SWEETNESS AND VITAMIN C.
3. INCLUDE HULLED STRAWBERRIES FOR THEIR FRESH FLAVOR AND ANTIOXIDANTS.
4. FOR A COOLER DRINK, ADD SOME ICE CUBES.
5. BLEND EVERYTHING UNTIL SMOOTH, ADJUSTING THE CONSISTENCY WITH A LITTLE WATER OR MORE COCONUT MILK IF NEEDED.
6. SERVE THE LECHE PINEAPPLE STRAWBERRY BLISS RIGHT AWAY, SAVORING THE REFRESHING MIX OF TROPICAL AND BERRY FLAVORS.

CREAMY CARROT APPLE DELIGHT

INGREDIENTS

- 1 CUP CARROTS, CHOPPED
- 1 LARGE APPLE, CORED AND CHOPPED
- 1 CUP RICE MILK
- 1 CUP SPINACH LEAVES

DIRECTIONS

1. CHOP THE CARROTS AND APPLE INTO BLENDABLE PIECES.
2. CLEAN THE SPINACH LEAVES WELL.
3. ADD CARROTS, APPLE, AND SPINACH TO A BLENDER, THEN POUR IN THE RICE MILK FOR A CREAMY TEXTURE.
4. BLEND UNTIL THE MIXTURE IS SMOOTH, ADDING MORE RICE MILK IF NEEDED FOR CONSISTENCY.
5. POUR INTO GLASSES AND SERVE RIGHT AWAY FOR A FRESH, NUTRITIOUS DRINK.

HONEYED YOGURT VEGGIE SMOOTHIE

INGREDIENTS

- 1 CUP PLAIN YOGURT
- 1/2 CUP MILK (YOUR CHOICE OF DAIRY OR PLANT-BASED)
- 1 TABLESPOON HONEY
- 1 CUP SPINACH LEAVES
- 1/2 CUCUMBER, CHOPPED

DIRECTIONS

1. COMBINE THE YOGURT AND MILK IN A BLENDER, CHOOSING ANY MILK THAT SUITS YOUR PREFERENCE FOR A RICH, CREAMY BASE.
2. ADD A TABLESPOON OF HONEY FOR NATURAL SWEETNESS.
3. WASH THE SPINACH LEAVES AND CHOP THE CUCUMBER BEFORE ADDING THEM TO THE BLENDER. THESE VEGGIES INTRODUCE A REFRESHING TASTE AND LOADS OF NUTRIENTS.
4. BLEND EVERYTHING UNTIL SMOOTH. IF IT'S TOO THICK, ADJUST BY ADDING A LITTLE MORE MILK.
5. ONCE SMOOTH, POUR THE SMOOTHIE INTO A GLASS.

CELERY CITRUS SPLASH

INGREDIENTS

- 2 CUPS CELERY, CHOPPED
- JUICE OF 2 ORANGES
- 1 GREEN APPLE, CORED AND SLICED
- 1/2 INCH PIECE OF FRESH GINGER, PEELED
- JUICE OF 1/2 LEMON

DIRECTIONS

1. PREP CELERY BY WASHING AND CHOPPING IT INTO SMALLER PIECES THAT ARE EASY TO JUICE OR BLEND.
2. SQUEEZE THE JUICE FROM THE ORANGES AND HALF A LEMON, CAPTURING THEIR VIBRANT CITRUS FLAVORS.
3. CORE AND SLICE THE GREEN APPLE, ADDING A CRISP, TART TASTE TO THE MIX.
4. PEEL AND SLICE THE GINGER FOR A HINT OF SPICE AND DIGESTIVE BENEFITS.
5. JUICE OR BLEND THE CELERY, GREEN APPLE, AND GINGER TOGETHER. IF USING A BLENDER, ADD A BIT OF WATER TO HELP THE PROCESS AND STRAIN AFTER FOR A SMOOTHER JUICE.
6. STIR IN THE FRESHLY SQUEEZED ORANGE AND LEMON JUICE TO THE CELERY BLEND, MIXING THOROUGHLY.
7. SERVE THE CELERY CITRUS SPLASH IMMEDIATELY, ENJOYING THE REFRESHING AND INVIGORATING COMBINATION OF FLAVORS.

SUNSHINE CITRUS BLEND

INGREDIENTS

- JUICE OF 3 ORANGES
- JUICE OF 2 LEMONS
- 1 TABLESPOON HONEY (OPTIONAL)
- ICE CUBES (OPTIONAL)
- MINT LEAVES FOR GARNISH (OPTIONAL)

DIRECTIONS

1. START BY SQUEEZING THE JUICE FROM THE ORANGES AND LEMONS INTO A LARGE PITCHER. THESE CITRUS FRUITS BRING A LOAD OF VITAMIN C, OFFERING A TART, REFRESHING TASTE.
2. STIR IN A TABLESPOON OF HONEY TO SWEETEN THE BLEND. THIS STEP IS OPTIONAL AND CAN BE ADJUSTED BASED ON YOUR PREFERENCE FOR SWEETNESS.
3. IF YOU PREFER YOUR DRINK CHILLED, ADD ICE CUBES DIRECTLY TO THE PITCHER OR TO INDIVIDUAL GLASSES WHEN SERVING.
4. MIX THE JUICE WELL TO ENSURE THE HONEY IS FULLY DISSOLVED AND THE FLAVORS ARE COMBINED.
5. SERVE THE SUNSHINE CITRUS BLEND IN GLASSES, OPTIONALLY GARNISHING WITH MINT LEAVES FOR AN EXTRA TOUCH OF FRESHNESS.

GREEN POWER SMOOTHIE

INGREDIENTS

- 1 CUP KALE, CHOPPED
- 1 CUP SPINACH
- 1 BANANA, SLICED
- 1 APPLE, CHOPPED
- 1 TABLESPOON CHIA SEEDS
- 1 CUP WATER OR ALMOND MILK

DIRECTIONS

1. RINSE AND PREPARE KALE, SPINACH, BANANA, AND APPLE.
2. COMBINE ALL INGREDIENTS IN A BLENDER, ADDING CHIA SEEDS AND YOUR CHOICE OF WATER OR ALMOND MILK FOR SMOOTHNESS.
3. BLEND UNTIL SMOOTH, ADJUSTING THE LIQUID AS NECESSARY FOR YOUR PREFERRED CONSISTENCY.
4. SERVE IMMEDIATELY FOR A FRESH, NUTRIENT-RICH BOOST.

COFFEE KICK SMOOTHIE

- 1 CUP COLD BREW COFFEE
- 1 BANANA, SLICED
- 1/2 CUP GREEK YOGURT
- 1 TABLESPOON ALMOND BUTTER
- 1 TEASPOON COCOA POWDER
- ICE CUBES
- HONEY OR MAPLE SYRUP, TO TASTE

1. START BY POURING THE COLD BREW COFFEE INTO A BLENDER. THIS WILL BE THE LIQUID BASE OF YOUR SMOOTHIE AND PROVIDE THE CAFFEINATED KICK.
2. ADD THE SLICED BANANA FOR NATURAL SWEETNESS AND A CREAMY TEXTURE.
3. INCLUDE THE GREEK YOGURT FOR A BOOST OF PROTEIN AND A SMOOTH CONSISTENCY.
4. SPOON IN THE ALMOND BUTTER FOR A NUTTY FLAVOR AND HEALTHY FATS.
5. SPRINKLE IN THE COCOA POWDER FOR A HINT OF CHOCOLATEY DEPTH.
6. ADD A FEW ICE CUBES TO CHILL AND THICKEN YOUR SMOOTHIE.
7. SWEETEN WITH HONEY OR MAPLE SYRUP ACCORDING TO YOUR PREFERENCE.
8. BLEND EVERYTHING UNTIL SMOOTH AND WELL-COMBINED. IF IT'S TOO THICK, YOU CAN ADD A LITTLE MORE COLD BREW COFFEE OR WATER TO ADJUST THE CONSISTENCY.
9. TASTE AND ADJUST THE SWEETNESS IF NEEDED, THEN BLEND AGAIN BRIEFLY.
10. SERVE THE COFFEE KICK SMOOTHIE IMMEDIATELY, ENJOYING A REFRESHING AND ENERGIZING BEVERAGE THAT'S PERFECT FOR BREAKFAST OR AN AFTERNOON BOOST.

GREEN TEA ZEN SMOOTHIE

- 1 CUP BREWED GREEN TEA, COOLED
- 1 RIPE AVOCADO
- 1/2 CUP SPINACH LEAVES
- 1/2 CUP FROZEN PINEAPPLE CHUNKS
- 1 TABLESPOON HONEY (OPTIONAL)

1. BREW GREEN TEA AND LET IT COOL.
2. COMBINE THE COOLED TEA, PEELED AND PITTED AVOCADO, SPINACH LEAVES, AND FROZEN PINEAPPLE IN A BLENDER.
3. ADD HONEY FOR SWEETNESS IF DESIRED.
4. BLEND UNTIL SMOOTH, ADDING MORE TEA IF NEEDED FOR A THINNER CONSISTENCY.
5. SERVE THE GREEN TEA ZEN SMOOTHIE IMMEDIATELY FOR A REFRESHING, NUTRIENT-PACKED DRINK.

TOMATO BASIL BLISS SMOOTHIE

- 1 CUP TOMATO JUICE (FRESHLY BLENDED TOMATOES OR STORE-BOUGHT PURE TOMATO JUICE)
- 1/2 CUP CELERY, CHOPPED
- A HANDFUL OF FRESH BASIL LEAVES
- 1/2 CUCUMBER, CHOPPED
- JUICE OF 1/2 LEMON
- SALT AND PEPPER TO TASTE
- ICE CUBES (OPTIONAL)

1. IF USING FRESH TOMATOES, BLEND THEM UNTIL SMOOTH TO MAKE 1 CUP OF TOMATO JUICE.
2. ADD THE TOMATO JUICE, CHOPPED CELERY, AND CUCUMBER TO A BLENDER. THESE INGREDIENTS WILL PROVIDE A REFRESHING BASE WITH A MIX OF FLAVORS AND NUTRIENTS.
3. INCORPORATE A HANDFUL OF FRESH BASIL LEAVES FOR A FRAGRANT, HERBY TOUCH.
4. SQUEEZE IN THE JUICE OF HALF A LEMON FOR A CITRUSY ZING.
5. SEASON WITH A PINCH OF SALT AND PEPPER ACCORDING TO YOUR PREFERENCE.
6. ADD ICE CUBES IF YOU PREFER YOUR SMOOTHIE CHILLED.
7. BLEND EVERYTHING UNTIL SMOOTH. IF IT'S TOO THICK, YOU CAN ADD A LITTLE WATER TO ADJUST THE CONSISTENCY.
8. TASTE AND ADJUST THE SEASONING, IF NECESSARY, THEN BLEND AGAIN BRIEFLY.
9. SERVE THE TOMATO BASIL BLISS SMOOTHIE IMMEDIATELY, ENJOYING THE SAVORY BLEND OF FRESH GARDEN FLAVORS.

ARUGULA ALMOND BLISS SMOOTHIE

INGREDIENTS

- 1 CUP ARUGULA LEAVES
- 1 RIPE BANANA, SLICED
- 1/2 CUP UNSWEETENED ALMOND MILK
- 1/4 CUP GREEK YOGURT
- 1 TABLESPOON ALMOND BUTTER
- 1 TEASPOON HONEY (OPTIONAL)
- ICE CUBES (OPTIONAL)

DIRECTIONS

1. WASH ARUGULA AND SLICE THE BANANA.
2. COMBINE ARUGULA, BANANA, ALMOND MILK, GREEK YOGURT, AND ALMOND BUTTER IN A BLENDER. ADD HONEY FOR SWEETNESS IF DESIRED.
3. BLEND UNTIL SMOOTH, ADDING ICE FOR CHILLNESS IF YOU LIKE.
4. ADJUST THICKNESS WITH MORE ALMOND MILK IF NECESSARY.
5. SERVE THE SMOOTHIE IMMEDIATELY FOR A FRESH, PEPPERY, AND SWEET NUTRIENT BOOST.

ARTICHOKE HEART REFRESH

- 2 COOKED ARTICHOKE HEARTS (CANNED OR STEAMED UNTIL TENDER)
- 1 APPLE, CORED AND SLICED
- 1/2 LEMON, JUICE EXTRACTED
- 1 TEASPOON OF HONEY (OPTIONAL)
- 1 CUP OF WATER OR VEGETABLE BROTH

1. IF USING CANNED ARTICHOKE HEARTS, RINSE THEM WELL TO REMOVE ANY BRINE. IF STEAMING FRESH ARTICHOKES, ALLOW THEM TO COOL AND THEN EXTRACT THE HEARTS.
2. CORE AND SLICE THE APPLE. APPLES ADD A NATURAL SWEETNESS AND FIBER.
3. SQUEEZE THE JUICE FROM HALF A LEMON, READY TO BLEND.
4. PLACE ARTICHOKE HEARTS, APPLE SLICES, LEMON JUICE, AND HONEY (IF USING) INTO A BLENDER. THE HONEY CAN ADD A BIT OF SWEETNESS TO COUNTER THE ARTICHOKE'S NATURAL BITTERNESS.
5. ADD WATER OR VEGETABLE BROTH TO HELP BLEND SMOOTHLY. WATER WILL MAKE IT LIGHTER, WHILE VEGETABLE BROTH CAN ADD DEPTH TO THE FLAVOR.
6. BLEND ALL INGREDIENTS UNTIL THE MIXTURE IS SMOOTH. FOR A JUICE-LIKE CONSISTENCY, YOU MIGHT WANT TO STRAIN THE BLEND TO REMOVE ANY PULP.
7. SERVE THE ARTICHOKE HEART REFRESH IMMEDIATELY, ENJOYING ITS UNIQUE, HEALTHFUL TASTE.

CLASSIC APPLE JUICE

- 4 LARGE APPLES (FUJI, GALA FOR SWEET; GRANNY SMITH FOR TART)
- 1/2 LEMON, JUICED (OPTIONAL)
- WATER (IF NEEDED)
- ICE (FOR SERVING)

1. WASH AND QUARTER THE APPLES, REMOVING THE CORES.
2. JUICE THE APPLES USING A JUICER, OR BLEND THEM AND THEN STRAIN THE MIXTURE FOR A CLEAR JUICE.
3. ADD LEMON JUICE TO ENHANCE FLAVOR AND PREVENT COLOR CHANGE.
4. IF THE JUICE IS TOO THICK, DILUTE WITH A BIT OF WATER TO TASTE.
5. SERVE CHILLED WITH ICE.

BERRY MINT CUCUMBER JUICE

INGREDIENTS

- 2 LARGE CUCUMBERS, CHOPPED
- 1 CUP MIXED BERRIES (SUCH AS STRAWBERRIES, BLUEBERRIES, RASPBERRIES)
- A HANDFUL OF FRESH MINT LEAVES
- JUICE OF 1 LIME
- 1 TABLESPOON HONEY (OPTIONAL)
- WATER (IF NEEDED FOR BLENDING)
- ICE CUBES (FOR SERVING)

DIRECTIONS

1. RINSE CUCUMBERS, MIXED BERRIES, AND MINT LEAVES UNDER COLD WATER.
2. PLACE THE CUCUMBERS, BERRIES, MINT LEAVES, AND LIME JUICE INTO A BLENDER. FOR A TOUCH OF SWEETNESS, ADD HONEY TO YOUR LIKING.
3. BLEND THE MIXTURE UNTIL SMOOTH. ADD A SPLASH OF WATER IF THE BLEND IS TOO THICK FOR YOUR PREFERENCE.
4. FOR A SMOOTHER JUICE, STRAIN THE BLEND TO REMOVE SOLIDS, USING A SIEVE OR CHEESECLOTH.
5. SERVE THE JUICE OVER ICE IN GLASSES FOR AN INSTANT CHILL.
6. ENJOY IMMEDIATELY, SAVORING THE REFRESHING AND ANTIOXIDANT-RICH FLAVORS OF THIS UNIQUE DRINK.